Personalisation in
Social Work

Personalisation in Social Work

ALI GARDNER

Series Editors: Jonathan Parker and Greta Bradley

LearningMatters

Published in 2011 by Learning Matters Ltd.

British Library Cataloguing in Publication Data
A CIP record for this book is available from the British Library.

ISBN: 978 1 84445 732 8

This book is also available in the following formats:
Adobe ebook ISBN: 978 1 84445 734 2
EPUB ebook ISBN: 978 1 84445 733 5
Kindle ISBN: 978 1 84445 735 9

Cover and text design by Code 5 Design Associates Ltd
Project management by Deer Park Productions
Typeset by Pantek Arts Ltd, Maidstone, Kent
Printed and bound in Great Britain by Bell & Bain Ltd, Glasgow

Learning Matters Ltd
20 Cathedral Yard
Exeter EX1 1HB
Tel: 01392 215560
info@learningmatters.co.uk
www.learningmatters.co.uk

Mixed Sources
Product group from well-managed
forests and other controlled sources
www.fsc.org Cert no. TT-COC-002769
© 1996 Forest Stewardship Council
FSC

Contents

Series Editors' Preface

The Western world including the UK and England face numerous challenges over forthcoming years. These include dealing with the impact of an increasingly ageing population, with its attendant social care needs and working with the financial implications that such a changing demography brings. At the other end of the life-span the need for high-quality child care, welfare and safeguarding services have been highlighted as society develops and responds to a changing complexion.

Migration has developed as a global phenomenon and we now live and work with the implications of international issues in our everyday and local lives. Often these issues influence how we construct our social services and determine what services we need to offer. It is likely that as a social worker you will work with a diverse range of people throughout your career, many of whom have experienced significant, even traumatic, events that require a professional and caring response. As well as working with individuals, however, you may be required to respond to the needs of a particular community disadvantaged by world events or excluded within local communities because of assumptions made about them.

The importance of social work education came to the fore again following the inquiry into the death of baby Peter and the subsequent report from the Social Work Task Force set up in its aftermath. However, it is timely to reconsider elements of social work education – indeed, we should view this as a continual striving for excellence – as this allows us to focus clearly on what knowledge is useful to engage with in learning to be a social worker.

The books in this series respond to the agendas driven by changes brought about by professional body, government and disciplinary review. They aim to build on and offer introductory texts based on up-to-date knowledge and to help communicate this in an accessible way, preparing the ground for future study as you develop your social work career. The books are written by people passionate about social work and social services and aim to instil that passion in others. The current text introduces you to the personalisation agenda in current social work practice, the values that underpin it and how it might shift the balance of power in adult social care. The voices of people who use social care services are included in this text, making real some of the core elements of personalisation that include being heard, taking risks and making decisions together with professionals but in the driving seat. The knowledge introduced in this book is important for all social workers in all fields of practice, not just adult social care, as they seek to reaffirm social work's commitment to those it serves.

Professor Jonathan Parker, Bournemouth University

Greta Bradley, University of York

Acknowledgements

I would like to thank three people who shared their time, stories and kindness to make this book possible. These three people demonstrate the possibilities of personalisation and their determination is something to be admired. I would also like to thank all my colleagues in the social work department at Manchester Metropolitan University for all their support and encouragement. In particular I would like to thank my colleague Barbara Tisdall for her contribution to the book and the time she has given to me throughout this process. I would also like to thank Ken Stapleton for sharing his abundance of knowledge and his infectious enthusiasm and positivity towards personalisation.

Finally I would like to thank my family, Des, Dad and Sue for their patience and proof reading and last, but not least, my two special stars Grace and Hope for giving me time off to write this book.

Introduction

This book is written primarily for social work students to improve their understanding of the personalisation agenda. It will support students in developing their practice in a way that embeds the ideologies, values, principles, theories, policies and processes informing this agenda. A central focus to this book is a belief that personalisation is about thinking and doing. The reader will be continually encouraged to consider their own underlying assumptions and values in relation to notions of social care and welfare. In addition to highlighting several success stories through service user narrative, the book will explore some of the challenges and dilemmas social workers are likely to encounter in supporting service users to direct their own support. This fundamental understanding and critical reflection will enable the reader to develop congruence between values and social work practice at all times.

It is fundamentally important that practitioners understand why and how this working context has emerged. The book provides a brief historical sweep of welfare in Britain leading up to the government's commitment to this agenda in the form of the *Putting People First* concordat (DH, 2007a). The reader will be encouraged to critically analyse and evaluate how changing policies and practices are likely to impact on their own role as practitioners as the personalisation agenda unfolds.

The book will support qualifying students to make the transition from theory to practice. Chapter 7 focuses on preparing for practice and provides a number of useful resources and activities helping students to develop their practice within a personalisation context. The book acknowledges that the establishment of the *National Occupational Standards for Social Work* (TOPSS, 2002), which describes the key roles for social work, precedes the development of the personalisation agenda. Some of the language therefore used to describe social work tasks and functions can appear somewhat outdated within a personalisation context. For example, there is a shift away from the social work role being described as one of 'manager' within the social work key roles to that of an 'enabler' within the self-directed support model. The book, however, will support the reader to see that values, theories and methods underpinning the personalisation agenda are very familiar to social work. Good practice has always involved putting the individual first and values such as respect and self-determination have also been adopted as key philosophies for social workers (BASW, 2002). Building on this assumption the text will support students in considering how to evidence their practice while on placement by working methodically through the social work key roles within a personalisation framework. In this way the book will also be useful to practice educators supporting students working in environments where personalisation and self-directed support are central to their work.

The book may also support qualified practitioners working in new personalised environments to reflect critically on their own practice. Several of the activities provided encourage the reader to return to the fundamental values of social work. In this sense the book provides opportunities for qualified social workers to consider the extent to which their own practice and values have been shaped by traditional models of social care and welfare. Chapters 2 and 3 offer an opportunity to reflect on the transition from care management to self-directed support and explore the subtle, yet significant, ideological differences in these two approaches.

The book can be used at many different levels. First, it can be used to simply understand how and why the personalisation agenda emerged. It can also be used to learn or familiarise oneself with new ways of working by reflecting on examples of existing practice and developments. The book, however, can also be used to encourage students and practitioners to engage with more radical forms of learning by challenging practice at a more fundamental level and addressing issues within an anti-discriminatory and anti-oppressive framework of practice.

Book structure

Chapter 1: Personalisation – Where did it come from?

The first chapter will trace the influences leading to the emergence of the current agenda. This will include an analytical examination of the history of social welfare. The chapter will reflect on the impact of the user-led movements and its influence in relation to emerging legislation and policy relating to self-directed support. By the end of this chapter you will have a clearer understanding of the policy and service delivery context within which personalisation now exists.

Chapter 2: Personalisation – A value base for practice

The focus of this chapter is to develop congruence between social work values and social work practice. The book will consider concepts of paternalism versus citizenship and the deserving versus the undeserving in relation to models of social welfare. The chapter will consider how anti-discriminatory and anti-oppressive models of practice can be developed within a personalisation context. Finally, the chapter will pose the question: is personalisation a new paradigm or simply a repackaged model of social welfare?

Chapter 3: The social work process and role

This chapter will focus on the actual process of securing a personal/individual budget. The chapter will provide knowledge in relation to the role of the social worker in enabling service users to direct their own support. It will focus on key stages of self-assessment, the resource allocation system, support planning and review. A range of case examples and student exercises will be provided to allow the reader to develop their knowledge and skills in this area. Emerging literature in relation to the future of social work in light of personalisation will provide students with opportunities to consider how social work fits into this agenda.

Chapter 4: Service user groups and personalisation

In this chapter we consider current practice and developments within different service user groups. This will include:

- key statistics in relation to current uptake;

- good examples of practice;

- obstacles and challenges;

- research summaries.

Chapter 5: Service user narrative

This chapter provides an opportunity to learn from three individuals who have used personal and individual budgets. The aim of the chapter is to reflect on their individual and collective experiences. The purpose of using the three individual accounts is to provide some insight into the diverse ways individuals have designed and managed their support. Activities will be used to support students to reflect on both the diverse and common experiences of individuals. The chapter will encourage the reader to think about the social work role in supporting people to use their own expertise to control and direct their support.

Chapter 6: Balancing rights and risks in self-directed support

The chapter addresses some of the key tensions that exist for service users, practitioners, managers and the government in promoting choice and control while reducing risk and harm. The chapter will explore both the ideological and practical debates surrounding the safeguarding agenda. Case examples and activities will be used to aid debate, learning and challenge in relation to this discourse. The chapter will reflect on emerging research in relation to safeguarding and personalisation and encourage the reader to evaluate findings critically.

Chapter 7: Preparing for practice

This chapter will focus on supporting students, academics and practice educators to understand the personalisation agenda within the Key Roles for Social Work specified within the *National Occupational Standards* (TOPSS, 2002) *and the GSCC Code of Practice for Social Workers* (GSCC, 2002). Mapping the social work key roles to the personalisation agenda will enable students to identify, analyse and demonstrate competent practice. In addition the chapter will consider the changing role of the social worker. Activities will be used to support students to look at the tasks and functions required of the contemporary social worker. The chapter will offer an opportunity to reflect on the evolving role of social work using research findings and commentary.

Learning features

As with other books in this series, case examples, activities, reflection points, research summaries and signposting to additional reading will be used to aid the learning process. The book is intended to be interactive. An understanding of personalisation requires a commitment to engaging with the values, theories, ideologies and histories that have influenced its development. As a student and a practitioner it is important that you are able and willing to reflect on your own thoughts, experiences and practices in a critical way (Jones, 2009; Quinney, 2006) but, more importantly, that you are willing to change fundamental assumptions, perceptions or beliefs and ultimately practice, as a result of that reflection.

Chapter 1

Personalisation – Where did it come from?

ACHIEVING A SOCIAL WORK DEGREE

This chapter will begin to help you meet the following National Occupational Standards.
Key Role 6: Demonstrate professional competence in social work practice.
• Review and update your own knowledge of legal, policy and procedural frameworks.
This chapter will also assist you to follow the GSCC (General Social Care Council) Codes of Practice for Social Care Employers.
Code 6: As a social care worker, you must be accountable for the quality of your work and take responsibility for maintaining and improving your knowledge and skills.
• 6.8 Undertaking relevant training to maintain and improve your knowledge and skills and contributing to the learning and development of others.

It will also introduce you to the following academic standard as set out in the 2008 social work subject benchmark statement.
5.1.2 The service delivery context.

Introduction

Personalisation was officially introduced in government policy in December 2007 with the publication of the *Putting people first* concordat (HM Government, 2007). It set out the shared aims and values required to guide the transformation of adult social care in order to transform people's experience of local support and services. Personalisation, however, is not specific to social care and started as a cross-government agenda in 2003. The emerging ideas were articulated in the 2004 Demos report, *Personalisation through participation: A new script for public services* (Leadbeater, 2004). In this report, author Charles Leadbeater described a society where service users would be placed at the heart of services, enabling them to become *participants in the design and delivery of services* (p. 19). He argued that by mobilising millions of people as co-producers of the public good they value, services will be more effective. He went on to identify five different meanings of personalisation.

• Providing people with customer-friendly versions of existing services.

• Giving people who use services more say in how these services are run, once they have access to them.

• Giving people who use services a more direct say in how money is spent on services.

• Enabling people who use services to become co-designers and co-producers of services.

• Enabling self-organisation by society.

Leadbeater (2004) describes the last two meanings as *deeper personalisation* in that it is not simply a matter of modifying services but challenging the ideology of the relationship between the state and the service users and changing whole systems of the way people work together. In his powerful concluding comments, these sentiments are very clear: *In an open, self organising society, government has to become molecular; it has to get into the bloodstream of society, not impose change or deliver solutions from outside* (Leadbeater, 2004, p. 89). While the Demos report was targeted at all areas of public policy, the opportunity and connections for social care to build on this platform of thinking were clear and went on to shape the policy and practice of social care from this point onwards.

Personalisation through participation embodied the sentiments of several different strands of ideology, theory, policy and practice throughout the history of social care. In order to understand this journey, a brief overview of the history is necessary to appreciate the following changes in social care.

- The relationship between service user and the state.

- The role of the state.

- The move from institutional to independent living.

- The voices of those using services.

- Policy, legislation and government thinking.

Perhaps the most comprehensive way to do this is for you to embark on a virtual journey and follow the timeline of social care thinking, policy and practice.

Nineteenth century

Social work first emerged as an activity around 1869 with the development of the Charity Organisation Society (COS) (Lewis, 1995; Glasby and Littlechild, 2009) with a belief that individual casework would be able to clearly assess whether a person was worthy or unworthy of assistance. The premise of its role lay in the fundamental belief that poverty was largely caused by individual and moral failings – by *fecklessness and thriftlessness.* COS officers would determine whether an individual was deserving or undeserving. Those deemed deserving would be eligible for charitable resources while those deemed undeserving would be sent to the workhouse. This professional role was made possible by the introduction of the Poor Law Amendment Act in 1834 which was driven by the government's determination to underpin the operation of its provisions with a clear ideological statement of the distinction between the deserving and undeserving (Englander, 1998).

Prior to the Amendment Act in 1834, local parishes had been the focus of the relief for the poor. In 1601 the Act of Elizabeth laid down that each parish was to be responsible for the maintenance of its own poor. The parish administered support to the poor which was funded by a compulsory poor rate levied at those living in the community (Marshall, 1985). In this sense the local parish was seen as a unit of government, and relief of the poor was not seen as an issue that central government should intervene in.

Around the early 1800s the cost of relief had been rising for between 30 and 40 years, yet the results were not improving. Disgruntled with the constant burden, in the early 1830s local taxpayers made their complaints known and outbreaks of rural violence made it clear that urgent reform was essential (Edsall, 1971). Opinion in Parliament, however, was divided as to how the Poor Law system could be improved. The main question preoccupying many members of Parliament was whether it was right for the state to take some responsibility in such matters.

The Poor Law Amendment Act of 1834 was introduced, taking the power out of the hands of the parishes and placing it into the hands of central authority. *It brought in professionalism in administration where there had been amateurism and it represented an uncompromising attitude to poverty* (Marshall, 1985, p. 23).

A key characteristic of the Poor Law Amendment Act 1934 was to make dependence on relief as unattractive as possible and it was hoped that the ultimate threat of incarceration in the oppressive Victorian workhouses would achieve this (Buck and Smith, 2003).

The realities of the workhouse were well documented to the community to ensure people did not become idle. Guardians of the workhouses were advised by the central authority to create settings that were *positively repellent* (Englander, 1998, p. 32). Rising at 5 a.m. followed by prayer, little food and hard labour then to bed at 8 p.m. meant conditions were tough and relentless. Mindful that some taxpayers might worry that building and running the workhouse would impose an expense on them, a self-financing 'pauper management plan' saw that all residents of the workhouse would have to work to pay off the cost of their maintenance. Local residents were also empowered to apprehend anybody found begging and to bring them to the workhouse. For their trouble, they would be paid 20 shillings, which would be added onto the account of the 'beggars tab' (Sandel, 2010, p. 36).

Resistance to the Poor Law and the regime of the workhouse started to emerge around the mid-1930s. At first in the north of England and largely on the back of the factory reform campaign, popular leaders adopted the resistance to the Poor Law as, essentially, one more aspect of a wider struggle (Edsall, 1971). Riots were commonplace as the working class showed their dissatisfaction and bitter resentment of the workhouse regime (Chinn, 1995).

ACTIVITY **1.1**

The terms 'deserving' and 'undeserving' were widely used in the nineteenth century to determine who should receive resources or services.

- *Do you think these terms are still part of current social work practice?*

- *Can you think of examples where people are still classified in this way either by the state or society?*

Continued

> **COMMENT**
>
> *It could be argued that there are still many examples where explicit or implicit discretion is used to decide whether a service should be provided. For example, an individual using drugs or alcohol presenting him/herself at Casualty on a busy Friday night may be treated with less compassion than a disabled person who has experienced a severe seizure, yet both could be presenting similar symptoms. In social work we like to think of ourselves as working in a non-judgemental way but it is likely that aspects of our work will be influenced by slotting people into categories of deserving and undeserving.*

1940s – The post-war years

The Poor Law was finally abolished in 1948 with the introduction of the welfare state along with the National Assistance Act 1948, establishing a national scheme of social security benefits and legislation to provide welfare services for older and disabled people. A key characteristic of this legislation was the distinction between financial support and welfare services. The National Assistance Act 1948 established a National Assistance Board to deal with the financial welfare governed by national rules while the responsibility of welfare services was delegated to local authorities. This separation was welcomed as it helped to remove the stigma of the old Poor Law and social workers could work with individuals without having to first determine whether they were deserving of that support (Jordan,1974, in Glasby and Littlechild, 2009).

Reflecting on this point, Glasby and Littlechild suggest that this attempt to distance social work from cash payments to those in need may be partly responsible for practitioners' subsequent failure to address poverty issues. This is potentially important in relation to the later development of direct payments and personal budgets which would call for social workers to re-engage with linking financial and welfare resources in supporting service users. Glasby and Littlechild (2009) suggest the involvement of social workers in making payments to service users is a fundamental shift in the nature of their profession and may go some way to explaining why some social services departments have been slow to take up direct payments.

Defining welfare

While it is difficult to define a welfare state precisely, the definition provided by Lowe (1999, in Powell and Hewitt, 2002) describes a welfare state as one which provides a minimum income to individuals and families, provides security to those falling into crisis and provides all citizens without distinction of status or class the best services available in relation to an agreed range of services. It was the universality of provision that made the welfare state something new and different. Prior to this, local welfare systems had varied from place to place. One of the key characteristics of the welfare state is the relationship it created between the state and the individual. The Beveridge report in 1942 firmly located the role of the state in administering and organising support and resources to individuals. At the same time welfare subjects were seen as citizens rather than paupers or non-citizens associated with the Poor Law (Marshall, 1963). It is interesting to note that this notion of citizenship was part of Beveridge's vision, as the Disabled People's Movement later criticised the government for creating a welfare system which denied their civil rights and failed to treat them as citizens. Further criticism, although from a different perspective, later came from right-wing critics who felt that the state should be 'rolled back' in favour of an 'opportunity state' whereby individuals would take more responsibility to create better conditions for themselves (Powell and Hewitt, 2002, p. 39). The question of how far a government should involve itself with such matters continues to divide government thinking.

ACTIVITY 1.2

- *Think about any aspect of the welfare state. You might choose health, social care, housing or education, for example.*

- *Try to identify both the advantages and disadvantages of the state being involved in your chosen example.*

- *You don't have to agree with all the reasons but it will help you develop an awareness of the economic, social and political perspectives that impact on social policy. For example, you might choose free school meals.*

Advantages

- *Good healthy meals provided for the child.*

- *Helps the child concentrate and achieve more out of education.*

- *Doesn't take money out of a tight family budget.*

- *Child will be more able to participate in sporting activities which will improve health and well-being.*

Disadvantages

- *The child feels stigmatised and is teased because of his/her social status.*

- *Disincentive for parents to provide healthy balanced diet.*

- *Child may be limited by choice – school meals cannot be tailored to his/her exact preference.*

- *Child grows up with the belief that the state will always provide – may limit aspirations.*

- *Costly exercise to administer for the government, local authority and school.*

COMMENT

The example you used probably demonstrated the complexities involved in deciding how far the state should intervene. You may have identified some clear benefits of state involvement but you may also have noted some negative consequences. In making decisions about the level of intervention, the government must balance several factors including financial impact and benefit, predicted outcome and not forgetting public perception in order to remain popular with the electorate.

The 1960s and 1970s

Out of the civil rights movement of the 1960s and 1970s, which questioned the way power was used and distributed in society, disabled people started to express their demand for social change by setting up organisations run by disabled people. Unconvinced that the state had shaken off the legacy of the old Poor Law and concerned that the state controlled and dictated how welfare resources were distributed, they sought to change medical-model-based thinking of disability (Swain et al., 1993). Disabled people characterised the old Poor Law as being an administrative model in their dealings with people with physical and other impairments, viewing them as a problem which required paid officials to assess, define, classify, register, administer and control. This is an important discussion, as the administrative model set the direction and tone for future disability policy and can still be viewed in current practice and policy (Davies, 1998).

In the early 1970s the Union of the Physically Impaired against Segregation (UPIAS) paved the way for a civil rights struggle when it redefined disability as a socially constructed phenomenon:

> *The disadvantage or restriction of ability caused by a contemporary social organisation which takes little or no account of people who have physical impairments and thus excludes them from participation in the mainstream of social activities.*

(UPIAS, 1976, p. 14)

Around the same time the antipsychiatry/mental health survivor movement was beginning to mobilise itself. Again critical of the medical model in mental health, service users campaigned in particular for the closure of long-stay psychiatric hospitals, another legacy of the old workhouse. This began to challenge existing perceptions of the institution as an appropriate model of care. A new piece of legislation, the Chronically Sick and Disabled Persons Act 1970, was introduced, placing a duty on local authorities to provide care and support services to disabled people to enable them to continue living in the community.

The 1980s

During the 1980s the Conservative government introduced a number of measures to tighten up the criteria for benefits in an attempt to eliminate the perceived 'dependency culture' and move to an individualistic, consumer-based approach to social care (McDonald, 2006). In 1981 the British Council of Disabled People (BCODP) was formed. Central to its strategy was the drive to increase the number of organisations controlled by disabled people. Viewing disability as a consequence of society's unwillingness to remove social barriers so disabled people could be equal citizens in mainstream social life, they set out to challenge the oppressive structures which stood in the way of their liberation.

The Social Security Act 1986 replaced Supplementary Benefit with Income Support, which had stricter eligibility criteria. In effect this piece of legislation financially disadvantaged many disabled people (Hudson, 1988). In response, the Disabled People's Movement successfully lobbied the government to introduce a new Independent Living

Fund (ILF) in 1988 for people on low incomes who had to pay for personal care. The fund was only ever intended as a five-year transitional payment for those directly affected by the changes in the benefit rules. Disabled people, however, reported greater autonomy and clearly favoured and publicised the positive effects of the Independent Living Fund (Kestenbaum, 1993). Threatened by the rising cost of the ILF, the government introduced new rules to the ILF in 1993, restricting its use to those under 66 with extensive care packages. The success of the ILF has continued to face subsequent governments with the dilemma of needing to prevent spiralling costs yet unable to ignore the fund's popularity with disabled people. Again in May 2010, the ILF rules changed, preventing access to the fund for any disabled person working less than 16 hours (Independent Living Fund, 2010). Disabled people, having had a taste of directing their own support, became more determined to bring about more permanent legislative changes to the system which would allow direct payments to become a viable option for those eligible for services.

The British Council for Disabled People was a key player in the campaign for direct payments and actively lobbied members of Parliament for their support in changing legislation (Leece and Bornat, 2006), particularly targeting the emerging Community Care legislation. Some local authorities started to experiment with different forms of payment schemes known as indirect payments, either via a voluntary organisation or via a trust fund. A nervous Conservative government reacted by explicitly stating in the guidance of the 1990 NHS and Community Care Act that current legislation prohibited the making of cash payments in place of arranging services (DH, 1990), much to the disappointment of the Disabled People's Movement, which then went on to increase pressure for specific legislation in this area.

The 1990s

The year 1990 saw the introduction of the NHS and Community Care Act (implemented in 1993) with a focus on market forces and the belief that support could be tailored to individual need if the concept of consumerism was embedded within the provision of social care. At the same time social service departments came under increasing pressure to tighten criteria and to target scarce resources to those with the greatest needs (Glasby and Littlechild, 2009). In reality there was a growing consensus that the focus of intervention was being pushed further towards crisis management with less space for promoting choice and independence.

The Independent Living Movement continued to lobby members of Parliament. This determined approach, along with a timely piece of research carried out by Zarb and Nadesh (1994), provided the extra push needed for a Conservative government dwindling in popularity to change direction. The government, which could not deny the accordance of principles underlying direct payments with their own neoliberal social and economic policies, was persuaded in 1994 to change legislation and make cash payments available to disabled people with effect from 1996 in the form of the Community Care (Direct Payments) Act 1996.

RESEARCH SUMMARY

Research carried out by Zarb and Nadesh (1994), Cashing in on independence?, remains a key piece of research in understanding the then Conservative government's decision to introduce legislation to enable cash payments to be made to individuals with an assessed need.

Seventy disabled people in England using direct or indirect payments to purchase their support were interviewed. The study found that:

- *It gave disabled people a greater degree of choice and control and higher levels of user satisfaction.*

- *Support arrangements funded through payment options were more likely to be reliable (and therefore more efficient) than directly provided services.*

- *More cost-efficient support arrangements financed by direct/indirect payments were found to be between 30 and 40 per cent cheaper than equivalent service-based support.*

COMMENT

While all three key findings may well have influenced the Conservative government, the attraction of providing services/support at a cheaper cost is likely to have played a significant role in finally persuading the government to legalise cash payments.

REFLECTION POINT

This is a good opportunity to reflect upon the impact that research findings can have on policy development. Sometimes we can lose sight of the connection between research and policy and practice changes.

As students it is important to keep up to date with current literature and use it to help you analyse its impact on how services, policy and practice have developed.

Inclusion movement and person-centred planning

The Independent Living Movement, led primarily by physically disabled adults, clearly focused on extending choice and control to give disabled people the opportunity to live more independent lives. At the same time, similar ideas were emerging in the learning disability arena. Theories of normalisation (Wolfensberger, 1972) and social role valorisation (Wolfensberger, 1983) linked to ordinary life principles had begun to influence policy development and service delivery. This work influenced ideas around person-centred thinking which John O'Brien brought to the UK, proposing that work with people with learning disabilities should be informed by the *five accomplishments of community presence; relationships; choice; competence and respect* (O'Brien, in Brown and Benson, 1992). Supported by professionals and user-led organisations, individuals and their families began to embrace this approach and build pressure and demand for services and support to be developed in this way. This has often been referred to as the 'inclusion movement' and was very popular as long-stay institutions closed down and people with learning disabilities returned to their communities as part of the resettlement programme in line with community care policies (DH, 1989). Since this time, person-centred practice (PCP) has been developed in this country by key supporters such as Helen Sanderson and Peter Kinsella. Described as a *process of continual listening, and learning: focused on what is important to someone now, and for the future* (Sanderson, 2000, p. 2), PCP has influenced the development of the personalisation agenda both in terms of its relevance to practice but more importantly its fundamental principles of sharing power and community inclusion (Sanderson, 2000). An understanding and appreciation of the convergence of the Independent Living Movement and the Inclusion Movement is important in understanding the influence and impact it had on subsequent policy development.

1996 – Community Care (Direct Payments) Act 1996

First, it is important to remind ourselves that personalisation is not just about direct payments, personal or individual budgets. It is also important to recognise the impact that direct payments legislation had in shifting policy thinking in relation to service delivery and social care generally. The 1996 Community Care (Direct Payments) Act came into force on 1 April 1997. It was described by Oliver and Sapey (1999, p. 175) as having *the potential for the most fundamental reorganisation of welfare for half a century.* The Act gave local authorities the power (not the duty) to make payments to disabled people aged between 18 and 65. The local authority had to satisfy itself that recipients consented to receiving the services and understood the financial and legal implications they were undertaking, often referred to as being 'able and willing'. Since this original Act in 1996 a number of changes have been made to extend the use of direct payments in terms of both those eligible and the breadth of how the payment can be used.

In 2000, new regulations extended the age limit for recipients of direct payments to include people aged 65 and over in England. Similarly, the Carers and Disabled Children Act 2000 extended the use of direct payments to carers, parents and carers of disabled children and disabled children aged 16 and 17.

Perhaps the clearest signal that the then Labour government intended to widen the use of direct payments came in 2001 with the introduction of the Health and Social Care Act. Under Section 57 of this Act, local authorities are required to offer direct payments to all eligible individuals (those with an assessed need under S47 of the NHS and Community Care Act 1990 and who consent to and are able to manage the payments with or without assistance).

At first, take-up for direct payments was slow and patchy across the country and the government recognised that significant changes were required (Glasby, 2009). As a result, new guidance was produced in 2003 (DH, 2003a) identifying key changes including the relaxing of rules around the employment of close relatives, allowing considera-tion of long-term benefits in assessing cost efficiency and the injection of a £9 million Direct Payments Development Fund (DPDF) in 2003 to pay voluntary organisations, in partnership with local authorities, to set up additional information and support services.

In addition, direct payments became one of the Social Services Performance Assessment Framework indicators (DH, 2003b), signalling a serious commitment to widening their use.

Finally, it is important to note the change of government in 1997. Labour came into power with a new perspective which became known as the Third Way, combining the free-market ideas of neoliberalism with notions of responsibility, along with an emphasis on independence and choice (Clarke, 2004). The White Paper *Modernising social services* (DH, 1998) identified the key priorities as promoting independence, improving consistency and providing convenient, user-centred services. In this sense the direction towards direct payments and personalised services became politically attractive to the key political parties.

Moving into the twenty-first century

Building on some of the key thinking around person-centred planning and the lack of strategic direction for learning disabilities services since the early 1970s, the publication of the White Paper *Valuing people: A new strategy for learning disability for the 21st century* in 2001 set out 11 objectives aimed at improving the lives of people with a learning disability. Based on four key principles of rights, choice, independence and inclusion, in many ways this White Paper is reflected in much of the thinking and practice later articulated as 'personalisation'. For example, person-centred planning was first formally adopted as government policy in this White Paper. It has since been included as a key method for delivering the personalisation objectives of the UK government's Putting People First programme for social care (DH, 2008b).

ACTIVITY *1.3*

Obtain a copy of the Valuing people *White Paper (2001), which can be found on the Department of Health website www.dh.gov.uk. You will find that this White Paper set out 11 objectives. Look carefully at objective 3:* Enabling people to have more control over their own lives. *Identify three ways in which people with learning disabilities can be supported to gain more control over their own lives.*

COMMENT

As you develop your understanding of the personalisation agenda and self-directed support, it will be interesting to note the links with your three answers above. Sometimes service users and professionals find it difficult to identify how services or support could help individuals gain more control over their lives because they are so used to traditional services such as day centres, respite care facilities, etc. As you will see in the following chapters, service users describe how some very creative yet simple solutions have led to them gaining more control. The case study below is one example of this.

Sally is a 24-year-old woman with mental health difficulties. She was unable to leave her home due to severe panic attacks. Sally lives alone and has no family and few friends to support her. She depended on daily visits from support workers to help her with personal care needs and to escort her to the shops, etc. Sally became very depressed as she wanted to have more time outside the house but depended on support. One of the support workers introduced Sally to her dog, which was a real success. Sally felt more relaxed around the dog and decided she would like to own her own dog to help her with her anxiety problems. Sally's social worker helped her complete a self-assessment and access an individual budget which she used to purchase a dog and to pay for dog food and dog training lessons. Six months later Sally goes out every day. She meets other dog walkers in the park and her anxiety levels have reduced dramatically. She now receives a weekly visit from support workers rather than daily visits. Sally says that Jesse (her dog) has helped her get her life back and she no longer has to depend on others.

The term 'personalisation' was starting to emerge as a frequent term in government circulars and White Papers. In 2005 a joint report by the Department for Work and Pensions (DWP), Department of Health and Department for Education and Skills was published: *Improving the life chances of disabled people.* In this report, the government recognised the benefit of personalising support through direct payments and committed to further research and development of individual budgets. Similarly in 2005, the DWP set out its strategy for supporting older people to achieve *active independence, quality* and *choice* in the services they receive in its report *Opportunity age* (DWP, 2005) and in 2006, the health White Paper, *Our health, our care, our say: A new direction for community services* (DH, 2006) described a *radical and sustained* shift in the way services were to be delivered. A commitment to ensuring that services were more personalised, whereby individuals had a stronger voice and became major drivers of service improvement, suggested that the government was about to embrace the notions of *deeper personalisation* that Leadbeater (2004) described in his new script for public services.

The White Paper of 2006 set targets to increase the use of direct payments and to develop and widen the extent of individual budgets whereby a variety of funds would be brought together. Individuals eligible would be offered a transparent sum which they may choose to take as cash or as a service or a mixture of the two, but with a common aim that it should offer them greater choice and flexibility (DH, 2006).

The ideas behind this White Paper in relation to individual budgets were heavily influenced by the work of In Control, a project set up in 2003 in order to find new ways of organising the social care system. In Control began to develop a model of working which promoted the concept of self-directed support, which led to the creation of the first individual budget. In Control began to offer support and advice to the government and local authorities around the idea and practice of individual budgets and self-directed support. In Control continues to be a key player in the development of self-directed support and it is worth spending some time accessing the resources on their website www.in-control.org.uk.

2007 and beyond

At the beginning of this chapter our journey started with the ministerial concordat, *Putting people first: A shared vision and commitment to the transformation of adult social care* (HM Government, 2007). In this document, the government set out four key areas in which individuals and communities may need support to ensure better quality services and choice and control in their lives. These areas are:

- universal services;
- early intervention and prevention;
- self-directed support;
- social capital.

Universal services

This refers to services that are important in everyone's lives to participate fully in their community. It refers not only to those people with care and support needs but provides a more inclusive approach to service delivery.

> **CASE STUDY**
>
> *Joan is a 75-year-old widow living in rural area with little social interaction. She is healthy and fit and until recently has been able to drive to visit friends and local groups. Since she has stopped driving she has become very isolated. There is a limited bus service and she has a considerable walk to the nearest bus stop. A local co-operative has developed a volunteer car project whereby journeys can be booked flexibly by individuals who pay a basic reasonable mileage cost. It is being used widely within this rural community, making it more cost-efficient and bringing the individual cost down for all those using the project. Joan's life has improved significantly since the development of this scheme.*

Early intervention and prevention

The second area refers to support available to assist people who need a little more help, at any stage in life, to stay independent for as long as possible. This may include help to safely maintain a home or training to get a job or return to work after a break.

> **CASE STUDY**
>
> *As part of a Return to Work strategy, a local council provides a mobile careers advice service which involves a bus visiting local areas. Residents can easily access the support and receive advice on career choices, completing application forms or making free phone calls to local employers. The mobile service is aimed at encouraging people who may be more reluctant to pay transport costs to get to a more central service or find it difficult due to illness or caring responsibilities.*

Self-directed support

This means having services available to meet people's needs rather than people having to fit in with the things on offer. It is about people who need support being able to choose who provides that support, and control when and where the services/support are provided.

CASE STUDY

Yusuf is a 19-year-old man with mental health problems. He lives at home with his mum, dad and two sisters. Yusuf has been offered weekly supported sports sessions at a local sports centre with a group of disabled people of a similar age. Yusuf has attended once and although he really enjoys sport he refused to return as he struggled with the amount of people and noise. Yusuf has now joined his personal budget with one other member whom he particularly likes. Between the two young men, they have enough money to employ a personal assistant to support them fortnightly with a sports activity which they choose alternately. The two young men have become good friends and are spending more time with each other outside this session.

Social capital

The fourth area of *Putting people first* is about society working to make sure everyone has the opportunity to be part of the community and experience friendships and care. It is about people becoming full members of the community. Social capital refers to engaging with people and showing them how they can influence the decisions that affect their lives.

CASE STUDY

A group of parents of adults with learning disabilities came together to work with the council to put ideas into practice to develop a telephone support line to support other parents in a similar position. The local council supported the group to grow through its own networks. The group has now developed a telephone support line which is operated by volunteers on a rotating basis which is manageable for all volunteers. The group of volunteers has now developed a social circle from this activity which has promoted their own health and well-being. The council fund this highly valued telephone support project and are responding to feedback at both a practice and strategic level in relation to future service delivery and developments.

Putting people first asserts that transformation of adult social care programmes should be co-produced, co-developed and co-evaluated and recognises that real change will only be achieved through the participation of users and carers at every stage (HM Government, 2007, p. 1). The example above is evidence of how parents and carers can be involved positively in each aspect of co-production from design, to implementation and evaluation. Research on co-production suggests that frontline workers should focus on people's abilities rather than seeing them as problems (Boyle *et al.*, 2006) so they are empowered to co-produce their own solutions to the difficulties that they are best placed to know about. The telephone support line is a good example of capitalising on strengths and skills rather than problematising a vocal group of parents who are trying to improve the system.

13

ACTIVITY 1.4

Visit the Department of Health website www.dh.gov.uk and search for 'Putting People First – the whole story'. Read the two-page document and write one sentence to sum up your understanding of the four areas of focus:

• *universal services;*

• *early intervention and prevention;*

• *choice and control;*

• *social capital.*

In pairs try to think of examples of how you might incorporate these four areas into your practice.

COMMENT

It is very important to think of personalisation in its broadest sense. Personal budgets have often been at the forefront of our minds when we think about personalisation but if we are to adopt the true essence of personalisation we need to think further than our work with individuals and consider how the community and society can contribute. It is only by thinking in this wider framework that we are likely to change our attitudes to welfare. Within a personalisation context this is essential if we are to shift the fundamental relationship between the state and the individual. If we can start to see individuals and communities as being capable of contributing in this way, we are more likely to place a higher value on their input and abilities.

The Social Work Task Force

In 2009 a report by the Social Work Task Force, *Building a safe confident future* (DH, 2009a), made proposals for the reform of social work over the next ten years including: the establishment of an independent National College of Social Work; an improved system of professional development, and a Licence to Practise for social workers. Leece and Leece (2010) suggest that the recommendations pose a contradiction to the personalisation agenda. On the one hand, concepts of personalisation and co-production are driving towards increased power and autonomy for individuals using services. The proposals contained within *Building a safe confident future,* on the other hand, intend to elevate social work to a new level of professionalism with a possible extension of power. It will be interesting to note whether these two agendas can coexist. The personalisation agenda calls for social workers to shift power over to service users in key stages of the process, including assessment, support planning and review. At the same time the safeguarding of vulnerable people is a key priority for the government as signalled by the Social Work Task Force (DH, 2009a). This in turn is likely to lead to increased regulation and social work presence in the lives of vulnerable people. Managers and social workers may struggle to make sense of these two policy contexts, which appear to be travelling in opposite directions.

Obtain a copy of the 2009 Social Work Task Force report, which you will find at www. dh.gov.uk. Read the executive summary of the report.

- *What do you think the key tensions will be for you as a social worker in supporting individuals to lead autonomous lives while ensuring you are being a responsible, accountable social worker?*

- *How might you deal with these tensions?*

COMMENT

Reading this report summary may have highlighted some of the tensions for you as a practitioner. As a social worker you will frequently come across situations where you have to balance your role as an enabler with one of protector. Within a personalisation context this can be even more challenging, especially given the current political climate in relation to the safeguarding of vulnerable children and adults.

The timeline has provided an overview of the historical, economic, social and political contexts that have shaped and influenced the development of the personalisation agenda. As demographics change, meaning increasing numbers of people living longer with more complex conditions such as dementia and chronic illness, current forms of welfare will also need to respond and change. By 2022, 20 per cent of the English population will be over 65. By 2027, the number of 85-year-olds will have increased by 60 per cent (HM Government, 2007). It is only as this agenda unfolds and evolves that we will be able to judge whether notions of self-determination and independent living can be embraced and adhered to in the process of transformation. Faced with finite resources and economic global downturn, there is a huge challenge to *build on best practice and replace paternalistic, reactive care of variable quality with a mainstream system focused on prevention, early intervention, enablement, and high quality personally tailored service,* as described in *Putting people first* (HM Government, 2007, p. 3).

2010 – A vision for adult social care

The new coalition government appears to be reinforcing a policy context which embraces personalisation, viewing it as central to social care improvement. The 2010 Local Authority Circular, *A vision for adult social care*, provides some clear messages that personalised services with clear outcomes will be expected in delivering social care in the future. Armed with slogans such as 'Big Society' and 'Think Local, Act Personal', government ministers are promoting notions of choice and flexibility through the increased use of personal budgets. While the principles behind personalisation appear to have been adopted by the current government, we will have to wait for the White Paper on long-term adult social care due to be published in 2011 to understand the details of just how it will be delivered and funded.

CHAPTER SUMMARY

This chapter has traced the history of social work and social welfare. When we study history we often look at important figures, groups, ideas and movements. We also need to be aware, however, of the process of history and think about how these events link together. Learning about history in this way helps us to understand why things are the way they are in the present and what might happen in the future.

It is important to understand the history of social welfare and the various influences that have led to personalisation as we know it today. The convergence of the independent and inclusive movements along with the need for governments to prepare for the demographic changes in the twenty-first century help us to understand why and how ideas get taken forward at the time they do.

While most human beings would agree that we should never return to the draconian methods of incarcerating the poor in workhouses as happened in the early nineteenth century, the impact of such historical events for individuals currently dependent on state welfare and support is a constant genuine reminder of why concepts of citizenship, individual control and autonomy must remain at the heart of social policy. Disabled people have been campaigning for many years for changes in policy which allow them to have more choice and control, yet it appears that those demands have only been acknowledged and responded to once the potential fiscal benefits of such a change can be realised. It is hard to imagine that some level of cost-benefit analysis is applied in developing social care policies. It would, however, be naive to think that changes in government direction occur only as a result of governments developing their understanding of the 'best' or 'fairest' way to treat people. The truth is it is probably a combination of both. In relation to personalisation, we have seen that many different drivers with varied priorities have managed to meet in the middle and may have found, at least in principle, a mutually acceptable way forward in the form of personalising services and support. It is only as we look back in history that we will be able to judge whether a system of personalisation contained the key ingredients required to deliver high-quality, individually tailored support at a cost acceptable to the public purse.

FURTHER READING

Englander, D (1998) *Poverty and the poor law reform in 19th century Britain, 1834–1914: From Chadwick to Booth.* Essex: Longman.

This book provides students with an opportunity to consider early developments of social work and social welfare as far back as 1834. It demonstrates the links between early nineteenth-century welfare provision to the development of modern-day social welfare. The book is accessible and interesting, bringing together history, policy, legislation and practice.

Powell, M and Hewitt, M (2002) *Welfare state and welfare change.* Buckingham: Open University Press.

The book provides a clear account of the nature of the contemporary welfare state and explores how and why the welfare state has changed in Britain throughout history. In this book Powell and Hewitt have explored the ideas and argument which have been advanced to explain the process of change. The book will enable students to appreciate and understand the broader context of policy and practice.

WEBSITES

www.scie.org.uk

An e-learning resource relating to personalisation can be found on this website providing more information in relation to the history and current developments and practice.

Chapter 2

Personalisation – A value base for practice

A C H I E V I N G   A   S O C I A L   W O R K   D E G R E E

This chapter will begin to help you meet the following National Occupational Standards.

Key role 1: Prepare for, and work with individuals, families, carers, groups and communities to assess their needs and circumstances.

* Work with individuals, families and carers, groups and communities to enable them to assess and make informed decisions about their needs, circumstances, risks, preferred options and resources.

Key role 6: Demonstrate professional competence in social work practice.

* Implement knowledge based social work models and methods to develop and improve your own practice.
* Work within principles and values underpinning social work practice.
* Critically reflect upon your own practice and performance using supervision and support systems.
* Identify and assess issues, dilemmas and conflicts that might affect your practice.
* Devise strategies to deal with ethical issues, dilemmas and conflicts.
* Reflect on outcomes.

Also important here are the General Social Care Council Codes of Practice for social care workers (GSCC, 2002), which state the following.

Social care workers must protect the rights and promote the interests of service users and carers. This includes:

* Treating each person as an individual (1.1).
* Respecting and, where appropriate, promoting the individual views and wishes of both service users and carers (1.2).
* Supporting service users' rights to control their lives and make informed choices about the services they receive (1.3).

As a social care worker, you must promote the independence of service users while protecting them as far as possible from danger or harm.

* Promoting the independence of service users and assisting them to understand and exercise their rights (3.1).
* Recognising and using responsibly the power that comes from your work with service users and carers (3.8).

The chapter will also introduce you to the following academic standards as set out in the 2008 social work subject benchmark statement.

4.6 Defining principles.
* **Values and ethics**.

Introduction

Personalisation is both a way of thinking and a way of doing. It cannot be viewed solely as a new system which social workers need to learn to operate. It must be understood at a more fundamental level which acknowledges the complex relationships social work and social welfare provision have with those who are in receipt of services. The importance of values in social work has long been accepted. There is increasing consensus that skills and knowledge are only a part of the process and that the way we filter information, make sense of it and use it to inform our actions is largely determined by our values. As Mullender and Ward (1991) state, *there is no such thing as value-free work, only workers who have not stopped to think what their values are.*

The underlying philosophy and principles guiding personalisation such as self-determination, dignity and choice must be fully understood by practitioners if they are to enable meaningful opportunities for individuals to direct their own support. We might assume that such familiar terms automatically inform the work of practitioners given that social work is committed to the following five basic values: human dignity and worth, social justice, service to humanity, integrity and competence (BASW, 2002). This somewhat dangerous assumption, however, ignores the complex factors impacting on our understanding and interpretation of these values.

In this sense social work values are never straightforward. They may change according to a situation; for example, a social worker's primary aim to care through supporting good parenting may quickly change to one of protection whereby actions have to be taken to remove a child or control a situation. Values may change over time whereby new research, understanding and debate influence change in policy or practice. Even within the relatively short time since the introduction of BASW's five basic values in 2002, social work landscapes have changed considerably. Influenced by serious case reviews and a rapidly changing political and economic context, our understanding and expectations of the social work role and process have shifted considerably. Today we are seeing increased pressure for social workers to assert more power in their role in relation to child protection following the death of Victoria Climbié in 2000 and Baby P in 2007. Similarly, depleting resources and changing demographics can influence notions of need. While social work may be fundamentally influenced and committed to certain core values, external influences such as those mentioned above will determine the extent to which these values can be realised and embedded within social work practice. In this sense values themselves cannot always be taken as absolutes.

One final influence on our values is public perception. Social work has increasingly found itself in the media spotlight, attracting public debate about how services should be funded, organised and implemented. Clearly, interest in the delivery of services which are publicly funded is a valid part of a democratic society and highly influential on the social care task. The collective beliefs about the 'right way' to provide for people's needs become embedded within societal perceptions and in turn inform the value base of social work.

Try to find a recent newspaper article or news report in relation to social work. This might be a child protection case, a report on asylum and immigration, an attack on a member of the public by a person with mental health problems, or local authorities allowing people to buy a football season ticket with their personal budget.

Here is one idea to get you started.

An article from the Manchester Evening News, *17 December 2007.*

NHS pays for season ticket
A SICK football fan was given NHS cash to buy a season ticket for a fellow supporter to keep him company at home matches.

This was the headline in a local paper referring to a man who used his individual budget to pay for his personal assistant to accompany him to football games. Without this support the service user would not be able to attend the football matches which had been a significant and valuable aspect of his social life prior to his disability. See if you can find similar headlines by searching the internet or maybe you can remember some that have appeared over time.

Discuss the issue with a partner and try to list the values underlying this report. Think about some of the following points.

• *Was the report positive or negative?*

• *Who was at fault or blame?*

• *Do you think your family or friends or the wider community would share a similar view?*

COMMENT

Reporting of social work-related issues is often presented in a way to evoke emotion and to encourage the reader to question the rights and wrongs of the case, particularly in the tabloid press. The public response to such articles affects the social work task in many ways. It gives government a sense of public opinion which may in part lead to legislative or policy changes. It also affects the people whom the articles are written about. In Chapter 5 service users provide us with an insight into public perception about their personal budget and the pressure it can put on them.

Values

One of the interesting features of our values is that we tend to adopt them unknowingly and stop recognising them as a key part of our practice. Thompson (2005, p. 11) suggests that *we tend to become so accustomed to our values and beliefs that we do not recognize that they are there or how they are influencing us. An important step, then, is to be clear about what our values are.*

In order to help us consider our value base in relation to the personalisation context, we will consider the concepts:

• paternalism;

• citizenship;

• social and medical models;

• partnership;

• anti-discriminatory practice;

• use of self in practice;

• empowerment.

But first we will take time to complete a short exercise that will inform our thinking in this chapter.

ACTIVITY **2.2**

• *On your own make list of as many words as you can associated with the word 'client'.*

• *Now make a list of as many words as you can associated with the term 'citizen/ citizenship'.*

If you are working with someone, share the lists and discuss the words you have associated with each term. Think about the following.

• *Did you use positive or negative words?*

• *Did you struggle to find words associated with either term?*

• *Have you ever been a client? If so, how did it feel?*

• *Do you or have you ever perceived yourself as a citizen? If so how did it feel?*

COMMENT

We will return to these words and their meaning later in the chapter but it will be useful to keep a note of your responses and see if your reading leads to you thinking about these concepts differently.

Paternalism

As discussed in Chapter 1, the development of the welfare state in 1948 paved the way for improved social and health care for many people in the UK. Embedded within this model of care was the assumption that the state would decide what and how to provide services to people in need. This saw the emergence of a paternalistic or 'nanny' state in which individuals in need relied on the expertise of the professionals to assess and provide the appropriate service.

The following quotation, taken from Minister Douglas Jay in 1937, illustrates the thinking of this time.

In the case of nutrition and health, just as in the case of education, the gentleman in Whitehall really does know better what is good for the people than the people know themselves.

(Jay, 1937, p. 317)

Personalisation rejects this paternalistic approach to social care and prefers to see the individual as better placed to make decisions about how their needs can be met. This change in direction, however, is no easy task for policy-makers, managers, social workers and providers. Deeply embedded paternalistic values developed throughout their training and rooted within their practice can make this a challenging shift. Social workers may need to examine their relationships with service users and realign their values, skills and practice in viewing people as experts in their own right rather than passive recipients of care. As Smale *et al.* (1993) suggest, changing practice requires workers to change the assumptions they make about individuals. This discussion then leads us to question the contribution or added value of social work. What expertise, if any, can social work offer in the process of assessment and service provision? In Chapter 3, we will explore this issue in more depth, where it will be argued that while social workers' roles may need to adjust in the way they relate and support service users, they do have a key role to offer in relation to enabling, navigating, advocating and promoting the rights and needs of service users.

Citizenship

What does it mean to be a citizen? In the exercise above you were asked to think about words you associated with 'citizen'. You might have suggested rights, entitlements, social inclusion, and liberty, among others. Marshall and Bottomore (1987) have widely contributed to our understanding of citizenship in a modern society. In their work, Marshall and Bottomore trace the development of citizenship, noting the significance of the end of the Poor Laws. Marshall and Bottomore define citizenship as a *status bestowed on those who are full members of a community. All who possess the status are equal with respect to their rights and duties which the status is endowed* (p. 18). Prior to 1918, those relying on poor relief in reality forfeited their civil rights of personal liberty by internment in the workhouse. This stigma, however, of depending on government support has been difficult to shake off and perhaps explains why notions of citizenship have continued to remain an aspiration rather than a reality for those in need of support. The sticking point is that service users continue to be seen essentially as having needs rather than being supported to exercise their rights. To be a citizen means having social rights and being included within society. Thompson (2005, p. 124) claims that *social work practice plays a pivotal role promoting or underpinning the citizenship status of particular individuals, families or groups who are otherwise prone to social exclusion.*

The Disabled People's Movement has been influential in promoting notions of citizenship, pointing out that disabled people's rights are often neglected as a result of social workers' focus on providing care services rather than on supporting the right to be able to participate in society (Oliver and Sapey, 1999). Duffy (2004, p. 9) claims:

today's human services have been built around the professional gift model of service delivery, which assumes that needy individuals will be given what they need by the professional who understand those needs.

Duffy (2006) describes the 'professional gift model' as being characterised by the *person in need* at the bottom of the chain relying on the professional to provide a service which has been funded by the government via taxation by the community. In this sense the person in need is more prone to be perceived by others and potentially themselves as *needy, reliant, tragic,* or *different* and grateful for the care or service that has been given. This reflects a paternalistic approach.

In contrast, Duffy (2003) describes the 'citizenship model' as promoting notions of rights and entitlements in the way agencies and professionals relate to individuals. The person is central to this process rather than simply being a recipient of care. The model recognises the individual engaging with their community at different levels, including: accessing support and services; choosing and directing support; making use of community activities and facilities and importantly contributing to that community. Duffy (2003) suggests that no one in society defines their life or their ambitions simply in terms of receiving social care. Duffy urges us to start thinking about the 'keys to citizenship': self-determination, direction, support, money, home, community life. While challenging social exclusion is fundamental in promoting and achieving citizenship, it also requires service users to be supported to actively contribute as citizens within their communities. In Chapter 3, we will explore the ways in which social work can support this process through self-assessment and support planning focusing on the keys to citizenship as defined by Duffy.

Our understanding of citizenship and its importance within a personalisation context is two-fold. First, our engagement with service users requires us to support social inclusion and, secondly, in challenging processes and attitudes which perpetuate marginalisation, stigmatisation and social exclusion. Not only is it important for an individual to feel like a citizen but they must be treated as a citizen too. In Marshall's analysis (1992), he referred to citizenship being *bestowed* on individuals, suggesting the importance of individuals being recognised and thus treated as citizens with equal rights. As described earlier, there is increased public and media interest and judgement in relation to who should and who should not receive welfare and on how that money should be spent, and arguably both can be linked to the concept of 'bestowing citizenship'.

It may be straightforward for society to understand and accept that public money can be used to pay for disabled people to live in a residential placement as they cannot look after themselves in their own home or attend a day centre which offers daily activities and companionship. It is perhaps not as easy for society to accept that someone may choose to take driving lessons to meet a social care need even if this happens to guarantee the best outcome.

Understandably there is public interest in how well the money has been spent. Unlike other evaluations of services, there is a somewhat curious approach to judging whether money has been spent wisely in social care. A satisfied taxpayer will often perceive value for money in social care if a disempowered, tragic and needy person is the result. This appears to reinforce the view that there was in fact a genuine need. It appears more difficult to perceive money as being well spent if the result is a healthy, empowered individual functioning well in society. One respondent in Henwood and Hudson's study (2007) commented, *we don't worry about all the money we waste on crap institutional provision, but we worry about giving someone £20.*

Phil is a 66-year-old man who lives alone, having recently lost his partner. Phil has a long history of mental health difficulties and always relied on his partner Tom to escort him when socialising outside the home. Phil's mental health significantly declined after the death of his partner of 20 years. Phil has not been out of the house much and relies on friends coming to the home for any social interaction. His social worker told him of a local drop-in, which he might benefit from, but Phil said this just wasn't for him. With some help from his social worker, Phil was able to identify his need to socialise with others outside the home to reduce his isolation. He was also able to identify bowling as one activity he had enjoyed with Tom. Phil was supported to get a small personal budget which he used to pay for a set of bowls and for a friend to support him for a month to enable him to feel comfortable getting to the bowling club and socialising with others. After four months Phil feels able to travel independently to the club. He has joined a team and plays weekly games. He is still reserved but does talk to a few members who are very supportive. Phil still has episodes of ill health but bowling is something he feels able to return to as soon as he is feeling in better health.

Judgements relating to value for money in social care appear to have somewhat different criteria compared with other public services. If extra money is given to a failing school which then improves its performance and achieves better results, we view this as money well spent. If social care money is spent on individuals leading more independent 'normal' lives whereby they can engage in ordinary, inclusive social, leisure, education and employment activities, it can often be assumed that the money was not actually needed in the first place and was not well spent.

Personalisation is not immune to public debate surrounding the 'deserving' and 'undeserving' and what society will tolerate and sanction. It is important, therefore, that social workers understand the complex conceptualisations involved in promoting choice and control at an individual level while promoting notions of citizenship by challenging social exclusion at a structural level.

A national study, Here to stay? *(Henwood and Hudson, 2007), used in-depth qualitative case studies to provide a detailed understanding of progress with self-directed support implementation. The study took place across three localities in the UK, at different stages of implementation. The sample included senior policy staff, commissioners, care managers, elected members and chief executives. It looked at ways in which people understood personalisation and their judgements about the desirability and feasibility of implementation. The study highlighted a variety of conceptualisations and judgements and found no ideological consensus in relation to self-directed support. Interestingly the study identified a number of ideological obstacles.*

Continued

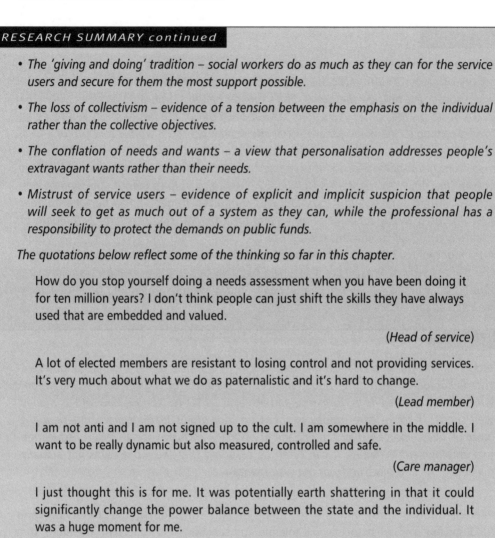

- *The 'giving and doing' tradition – social workers do as much as they can for the service users and secure for them the most support possible.*

- *The loss of collectivism – evidence of a tension between the emphasis on the individual rather than the collective objectives.*

- *The conflation of needs and wants – a view that personalisation addresses people's extravagant wants rather than their needs.*

- *Mistrust of service users – evidence of explicit and implicit suspicion that people will seek to get as much out of a system as they can, while the professional has a responsibility to protect the demands on public funds.*

The quotations below reflect some of the thinking so far in this chapter.

How do you stop yourself doing a needs assessment when you have been doing it for ten million years? I don't think people can just shift the skills they have always used that are embedded and valued.

(Head of service)

A lot of elected members are resistant to losing control and not providing services. It's very much about what we do as paternalistic and it's hard to change.

(Lead member)

I am not anti and I am not signed up to the cult. I am somewhere in the middle. I want to be really dynamic but also measured, controlled and safe.

(Care manager)

I just thought this is for me. It was potentially earth shattering in that it could significantly change the power balance between the state and the individual. It was a huge moment for me.

(Senior manager)

Social and medical models

It is worth noting the links between paternalism and citizenship in relation to the social and medical models of disability. The medical model has tended to focus on the physical limitations of the individual and views diagnosis as a starting point to dealing with illness and disability. The importance of understanding the cause of someone's illness or disability provides the key to work towards a cure, control or management. While some researchers such as Mackenzie (2005) and Watson (2003, cited in Grant *et al.*, 2005) claim merits in the medical model approach, the last 20 years have seen the emergence of a new paradigm for understanding disability: the social model.

The social model of disability emphasises the physical and attitudinal barriers that exclude a disabled person from participating fully in society (Oliver, 1990). Essentially the social model views disability as something society imposes upon a person. It acknowledges that while some people may have physical, sensory, intellectual or psychological variations, these impairments do not have to lead to a disability unless society fails to take account of these and adapt to ensure inclusion.

Both the medical and social models have been criticised for presenting somewhat simplistic views of their position in relation to disability (Barnes and Mercer, 2010). The complex nature of disability and impairment has been well documented and this debate cannot be covered fully in this text. It is important, however, to recognise a growing voice in disability politics which suggests that both the personal experience of impairment and the social exclusion imposed by a disabling society need to be acknowledged and integrated in a full analysis if we are to understand and respond to how disability and impairment operate. For many years the suppression of the subjective experience of impairment has been intentional in forcing governments and society to acknowledge the disabling barriers it creates. Crow, in Barnes and Mercer (1996), asserts that if all disabling barriers were removed, some people with impairments would still face disadvantage, for example limitations to an individual's health or their experiences of pain may constrain their participation in activities. Crow goes on to suggest that we need to acknowledge the experience of impairment, without underplaying the overwhelming scale of disability and that only then will we be able to achieve a route for change.

REFLECTION POINT

The professional gift model described above could be seen to reinforce medical model thinking in that the person is viewed as needy and that professional support will help manage the problem. In contrast, the citizenship model focuses on including the individual in directing support which can enable inclusion.

ACTIVITY 2.3

To illustrate the importance of underlying values in the way we perceive individuals, read the following information.

Omar is a 25-year-old disabled man who cannot meet any of his personal needs. He needs 24-hour support and will need two people to support him outside the home. He has challenging behaviour and becomes very aggressive if he doesn't get his own way. Omar uses no verbal communication and relies on others to interpret his needs.

Think about this extract of information. What picture do we have of Omar? What do we know about him? Reflecting on the chapter so far, answer the following.

* *Does this information reflect the medical or social model? (Discuss your answer in pairs. Think about how and why you have chosen the model.)*

* *Does this information describe a client or a citizen? (Discuss the difference with reference to the professional gift model and citizenship models.)*

Continued

> COMMENT
>
> *Hopefully you spotted that this information reinforces the medical model. It sees the problem resting with Omar. There is a negative focus on his needs and it fails to recognise that the environment or the way he is supported contributes to his disability.*

ACTIVITY **2.4**

Thinking about Omar using the social model, try to write a paragraph to describe his situation. Try to present Omar as a citizen.

> COMMENT
>
> *As social workers we sometimes forget to include service users' strengths as we focus on the problem or the weakness that has been identified in the referral. Sometimes the systems we work within can persuade or force us to adopt a medical model approach in order to access and secure services for service users. Social workers are always aware of the financial constraints they are working with and that resources are targeted at those deemed as most needy. It is important, however, to highlight and maximise service users' strengths and expertise wherever possible.*

The introduction of government guidance, the Fair Access to Care Services framework (FACS) (DH, 2003), set out to address inconsistencies across the country in relation to who gets support, in order to provide a fairer and more transparent system for the allocation of social care systems. It could be argued, however, that such inflexible screening and assessment systems, while attempting to standardise practice and offer transparency, leave little space for service users to be described within their own personal contexts in an inclusive manner. Henwood and Hudson (2008) suggest there is an inherent tension between FACS and the personalisation agenda in that:

> *the latter is based around self assessment, self determination, choice and individually geared support focused on a wide definition of health and well being. The former is reliant on tightly circumscribed categorisation, standardisation, consistency of treatment and explicit decision-making.*

There has been some government recognition of the shortcomings of FACS in relation to personalisation with the introduction of government guidance seeking to deliver a whole-system approach to eligibility (DH, 2010b). While it goes some way to acknowledging local community needs as well as individual needs, it still requires social workers to operate within rigid boundaries in deciding whether they have an eligible need and therefore become entitled to a resource.

There lies a complex maze of tensions for social workers to navigate. On the one hand, they have to work within a medical model framework which dictates criteria and allows little flexibility yet may lead to more resources. On the other hand, they are aware of the need to adopt a social model approach in which they should value and highlight the strengths and uniqueness of each person. The tensions between the social and medical models are not new to social work but the personalisation agenda does challenge this analysis further. This process is worthy of reflection as the model the practitioner adopts will inform their conceptualisation of the professional task.

To illustrate this we shall return to the example of Omar above. It is clear to see how our understanding and conceptualisation of this scenario influences the professional task. If we perceive Omar solely as a disabled person dependent on others to think and act for him, then our actions are also likely to reflect this perception. In our assessment our primary focus will be Omar's needs. In turn we are more likely to adopt a paternalistic approach in which we rely on our own expertise and professionalism to design a care plan that best meets his needs. In this sense we have understood Omar's situation and reacted to his situation within a medical model framework. If, however, we believe that there is more to Omar than the case notes suggest, we are likely to adopt a social model approach and try to understand why he is behaving in an aggressive manner and consider more creative ways of communicating with him to find out his wishes. In practice, an integration of both the medical and social models is required. The social worker understands the impairment while working to minimise or remove factors which disable the service user and limit their opportunities to participate and direct their own support.

Partnership working

So far we have tried to unravel some of the underlying values and theories influencing our practice as social workers. We now need to consider how we engage with service users, their families and other stakeholders in supporting individuals to direct their own support. The answer may appear simple: *we work in partnership*, and it is certainly easy to say we do this; but what does it actually mean to work in partnership?

Partnership between service users and professionals has long been established as a core component of social work practice. Legislation and government guidance have promoted the concept of partnership working in all aspects of social work from community care to child protection. Marsh and Fisher (1992) propose that the principles upon which partnership is practised include: user agreement, involvement, negotiated agreement and users having the greatest possible choice of the service offered. Pugh and De'Ath (1989, cited in Braye and Preston-Shoot, 2001) suggest partnership can be understood as a continuum from involvement in a decision through to the service user being in control of the process.

At its simplest level partnership working means working with service users and other agencies, rather than doing things for them, and this is a good starting point. Thompson (2006, p. 123) however, suggests that it requires:

> *...a degree of humility to accept that professionals do not have all the answers and clients have a major contribution to make in resolving the difficulties that have been identified.*

Although this quotation precedes the development of self-directed support, in many ways it captures the essence of personalisation. It steers social workers away from adopting the professional gift model and working within a paternalistic framework. Instead it recognises service users as having insight into their own needs. It views them as citizens with relationships and connections within families, networks and communities which only they fully understand. Many solutions and sometimes support can be found within these networks but the social worker must take the lead from the service user in unlocking this understanding.

The mandate for partnership working was introduced formally in the NHS and Community Care Act 1990 with an emphasis on consumer power. It was assumed that the inevitable outcome of the Act would be the ability of service users to express their choice and act upon it. Armed with clear guidance in relation to decision-making procedures, channels of complaint and involvement in assessment and planning, service users would be able to assert their own views on how best to meet their needs. While these conditions went some way to changing the working relationship between the service user and the professional, the absence of one key ingredient – cash – meant that true consumerism could never be achieved.

Arguably, Community Care failed to reject a paternalistic approach to social work with adults. As a result, the somewhat tame gestures of handing over power and control remained largely tokenistic. The framework and terminology, which at its time may have appeared radical and refreshing, actually only served to reinforce the belief that power remained securely with the social worker and the state. At second glance, however, shouldn't we have seen the writing on the wall? The clues may have been in the language used to describe this process: *care management*, *care manager* suggesting the need for someone to be in charge of care. At one level, care management claimed to be about *tailoring services to individual needs* yet at another level social workers were required to act as *gate keepers*, *secure service* and *support and control the delivery of the care plan*. *The role of the practitioner is to assist the user in making choices from these resources, and put together an individual care plan* (DH, 1991). The language used within care management suggests the values underpinning this process were based on a paternalistic model whereby the 'expert' care manager/social worker would support the service user to make 'sensible' decisions about how best to meet needs. One has to question how far we have journeyed from the sentiments of Minister Jay in 1937 in claiming that the *gentleman in Whitehall really does know better what is good for the people than the people know themselves* (Jay, 1937) – in reality, perhaps only as far as the *gentleman in the town hall*.

In contrast, the development of the personalisation agenda is based on a more radical form of partnership working which insists that power is transferred to the service user in relation to assessment, support planning and crucially the allocation of resources, the money. Its success is based on a model of citizenship which places the individual at the centre and encourages professionals and service users alike to work together in identifying natural, community and paid support rather than thinking purely in terms of services.

Finally, a word of caution in understanding partnership working. It would be naive to believe that intention alone will enable us to develop equal partnerships with service users. This assumption ignores the powerful structures and processes inherent within local authorities and society at large. Social workers must always acknowledge the power they hold in each interaction with a service user. No matter how much control we transfer to service users, the gatekeeping role of the social worker has not been removed. Social workers hold significant power at each point of the process whether it be access to resources or reviewing the outcome. Service users will be ever aware of this relationship and the risk it carries in terms of accessing or keeping a resource. The service users we will hear from in Chapter 5 clearly illustrate this point.

Anti-discriminatory and anti-oppressive practice

If we acknowledge the central role of power in both our relationships and the professional task of social work, we must also learn to recognise its presence and seek to reduce its impact wherever possible. In practice, power can be seen to operate at a personal and structural level. The status afforded to individuals is often something deeply embedded within our consciousness before we have even met an individual and will be informed by a range of factors including race, gender, class, etc. As social workers we often enter situations bringing a power which we may not even recognise. In addition, power can be derived through perceived threat; for example, a service user may perceive a visit from a social worker as intrinsically linked to imposing some control in their lives. Finally, structural power is ever present in that social workers often enter situations with a mandate potentially affording them powers to take controlling measures in a given situation. In this sense, social workers have considerable access to power over service users. Social workers must seek to make sure that they not only recognise discrimination and oppression in the lives of service users but ensure their own practice does not add to or exacerbate their oppression.

Social workers play a pivotal role between the state and its citizens. Every intervention can lead to either potential empowerment or potential oppression (Thompson, 2006). An understanding of anti-discriminatory practice and anti-oppressive practice is therefore essential. The difference between these two concepts has been a constant focus of debate. Thompson (2006, p. 13), claims the difference to be *primarily semantic rather than theoretical and ideological*, while others including Braye and Preston-Shoot (2001) resist these terms being used interchangeably. Braye suggests that anti-discriminatory practice is *reformist, challenging unfairness or inequity in how services are delivered, whereas anti-oppressive practice is more radical, seeking a fundamental change in power relationships* (p. 54).

In relation to personalisation, I would suggest that distinguishing between the two is important. In this context, anti-discriminatory practice is concerned with how we engage with service users and their families, designing processes which promote equality, widening access to resources, along with some of the basic prerequisites such as treating people with dignity and respect and promoting self-determination. Personalisation, however, requires a more radical approach to working with individuals, as we have seen above. Social workers need to develop an acute understanding of structural inequalities. They need an awareness of oppressive legal structures and practices and an appreciation of the histories and relationships that exist between those in receipt of services and those responsible for providing welfare. Only then will social workers fully appreciate the need to realign power relationships at a more fundamental level in order for them to be seen and treated as citizens able to lead change in their own lives. In this sense anti-oppressive practice is more concerned with challenging social constructs of need based only within a paternalistic model. It relies upon an alternative conceptualisation of individuals with rights and entitlements located within a citizenship model of thinking and practice.

An important feature of anti-oppressive practice is a requirement for social workers to be proactive in their work with service users. They must adopt a questioning approach and be willing to question underpinning knowledge and values informing policy, guidance and practice. Social workers in this sense see more than descriptions of individuals and their scenarios; they understand and analyse this information by locating it within wider social, geographical and political contexts. Social work then becomes a dynamic process whereby social workers develop creative ways of working. Burke and Harrison (2007, cited in Adams *et al.*, 2009) suggest that these ways of working, informed by a complex, critical, politicised and geographical view of our culturally plural society, will contribute to the development of relevant and appropriate services.

ACTIVITY **2.5**

This exercise will help you to develop your understanding of anti-discriminatory and anti-oppressive practice.

The Direct Payments Act 1996 states that all individuals with an assessed community care need are entitled to and should be offered the option of receiving a direct payment.

• *Consider the responses of the social workers A and B.*

Social worker A
'Yes Mr Walker, you have been assessed as having a community care need. You have two choices. You are entitled to a direct payment. This will be money given to you for you to spend as you choose. You will be responsible for employing someone and dealing with the money. It is quite a difficult process and a lot of older people find it very hard. Personally I don't agree with them but you can have one if you want. The other option is I could sort out some home care to come to you twice a day to help you to get out of bed in the morning and back in at night.'

Social worker B
'Yes Mr Walker, you have been assessed as having a community care need. It's really important that we work together to make sure you get the right support. I can tell you about your options so you can make the right choice for yourself. You are entitled to a direct payment. This is a system whereby the local authority will give you money so you can choose how to spend it. You can choose whether to employ an agency or a personal assistant perhaps. You can have support to help you with this process and I could ask someone from our local direct payments team to come and talk to you if this would help. I can leave this leaflet with you today which gives you examples of how other people have used direct payments. You may prefer to use our home care service to help you in the mornings and the evenings. I can organise this for you if you choose this option. It might be useful to have some time to think about it, read the leaflet and discuss it with your family. Have you any questions at this stage? I will come back in two days so we can talk again.'

Continued

ACTIVITY **2.5** *continued*

Now think about the difference between the two approaches by answering the following questions.

- *Identify examples of anti-discriminatory practice.*

- *Identify examples of anti-oppressive practice.*

- *Can you identify any values underpinning the practice of social worker A?*

- *Can you identify any values underpinning the practice of social worker B?*

COMMENT

Hopefully the exercise illustrated the importance of both anti-discriminatory practice and anti-oppressive practice as well as the difference. Social worker A probably fails to adopt either an anti-discriminatory approach or an anti-oppressive approach. While she does inform Mr Walker of his entitlement to a direct payment, she does not provide him with any information or confidence to take this option. Her connection with Mr Walker is based on the professional gift model, in that she is the expert, she knows what he needs and she can sort these out. In short, she tells Mr Walker what is going to happen. She also appears to be unaware of the power she holds in this exchange.

Social worker B, on the other hand, provides a fuller picture in relation to direct payments. First, she clearly tells Mr Walker about his entitlements. She provides him with additional information and gives him time to digest information and discuss it with his family. She appears to value Mr Walker's contribution and underlying this short exchange social worker B demonstrates respect and promotes self-determination. There is also an indication that she is aware of wider social and political contexts and the power she holds as a social worker. She gives Mr Walker time to consider his position, for him to reflect on the information. In doing so she is offering meaningful potential for him to make an informed decision and lead the way in directing his own support. At the same time she reassures him that she will support him to make the right decision. In this brief exchange we return to the words of Thompson (2006). Every intervention can lead to either potential empowerment or potential oppression.

Self and practice

It would be an impossible task to do social work without connecting in some way to the values and principles that underpin practice. While many jobs require the ability to analyse and interpret information, social work requires a personal engagement at a deeper level. The use of self in practice is almost inescapable. At times most social workers would probably like to take a break from the constant questioning and professional and personal dilemmas they are faced with. This is made all the more difficult as assessments, decisions and interventions can lead to significant changes or consequences in another individual's life. We only have to think about the dilemmas social workers face in deciding whether a child is at 'significant risk of harm' or whether a person with mental health problems should be compulsorily detained. The ability to understand, interpret, analyse, consolidate, reflect and review information is central to the role of a good social work practitioner.

To help you think about the use of self in social work practice, consider the following analogy.

Reg has just started a car mechanic apprenticeship. On day one the boss gives Reg his own toolkit and tells him how each tool works and when it should be used. By the end of his training he assures Reg that he will know all the tools well and will be able to make decisions about when to use them. He will also be shown how to make sure all his tools are in good and safe working order.

Social work students might be given some basic information about the course on day one such as a timetable and an assessment schedule. They will also have to fill in lots of forms and probably pay out more money for various registrations, but what about a toolkit? Social work students will quickly come to realise that they already have a toolkit – a virtual toolkit, the self. In the same way as the car mechanic, Reg, the social worker will need to learn about the toolkit and the individual tools. In order to use the tools effectively, social work students will also absorb knowledge and experience as part of the course. Once new information or an experience is taken in, trainee social workers will start to use their interpreting tools. The knowledge they have recently acquired is only part of the picture as our personal values informed by our biographies, past experiences and cultural norms begin to filter what is seen, begin to make sense of it and evaluate its worth. As we saw at the beginning of the chapter, Mullender and Ward (1991) suggested that there is no such thing as value-free practice.

The acceptance of the self in practice is the key starting point for all social work students. Braye (2001) suggests that the ability to learn, unlearn and relearn is vital to social care practice. The ability to recognise when and how we connect with new information and knowledge is fundamental in beginning to fine-tune our tools so we are ready for practice. As a social work student on your first home visit or as a practitioner, you might imagine your virtual toolkit: remember to check that your tools have been well conditioned before your visit and make sure you don't leave them in the back of the car!

Critical practice

If we acknowledge that knowledge, skills, experience and values play a significant part in social work practice, we need to make sure that we continually monitor and self-regulate our thoughts, beliefs, decisions and actions. Jones (2009) states the importance of students being reflective and reflexive within their practice. Students must learn to analyse professional activity during or after an event. Jones goes on to suggest that students should use supervision or discussions with colleagues to gain a deeper understanding of an experience which in turn will improve practice. Schön (1986) describes reflection as being both in-action (i.e. when we are immersed in a situation) and on-action (i.e. after the event when we can rewind situations and be more retrospective). In addition to being reflective, social workers need to adopt a reflexive approach to their practice. Reflexivity is different from reflection as it involves challenging and critiquing oneself at a broader level. Jones (2009, p. 98) claims reflexive practice *causes us to evaluate our position within our practice from a personal involvement perspective*. Webb (2006, p. 36, cited in Jones, 2009) provides a more radical definition of reflexivity, stating that:

A reflexive practitioner is engaged in radical confrontation with the very ethical basis and legitimation of practice and self involvement, introducing an important moral dimension into social work that is lacking in the reflective practice literature.

In relation to personalisation, I would suggest the more radical activity of reflexivity is essential. Throughout this chapter we have explored the importance of realigning fundamental social work values in order to see people as experts in their own lives. Practitioners must recognise and examine the complex relationships social work and social welfare have had with those in receipt of services. It is only by critically drawing on the histories and biographies of marginalised groups that we can fully appreciate and develop new ways of working with service users based on this new paradigm. For example, the history of personalisation needs to include an understanding of the position of disabled people and the emergence of the Disabled People's Movement. The campaigns based on the insistence by disabled people to be treated as citizens with rights and entitlements are central to a self-directed model of support. Clearly it is important that practitioners reflect on their practice and continually analyse the professional task and their relationships with service users. However, the ability to be reflexive and challenge not only oneself but the ethical basis of practice (Webb, 2006, cited in Jones, 2009) is more likely to lead to a longer-lasting commitment to the core principles underlying professional practice.

Empowerment

The term 'empowerment' is familiar to all practitioners, but do we ever give enough time to think about what it means? We might suggest that empowerment is about giving power back to service users or enabling people to make decisions or take actions to improve their lives. This is part of the process, but unless we recognise that it is about more than facilitating or enabling people to do things then it is unlikely that the changes individuals make will have a long-lasting effect or benefit to their life. This type of support may, perhaps, help people to function better in their day-to-day life, or improve their interpersonal relationships. Professionals, however, must encourage service users to understand the connections between their own circumstances and the broader socio-political context in which they exist. Professionals and service users must take seriously the significance of disadvantage and oppression that service users face in everyday life. It is a matter of connecting the personal with the political and from a service user perspective, using this insight to motivate oneself to make decisions and changes which are likely to have a lasting effect. The belief of the necessity to take an action becomes more important than the ability to take the action as the individual develops an internal compass which can navigate them through complex situations and decisions. Service users begin to take control of their lives and work in a way which alters existing power relations between themselves and professionals or agencies rather than working within them. This radical rather than functionalist approach to problem-solving is based on a combination of cognitive and emotional factors which is more likely to equip service users with the confidence and skills to demand services and support based on what they want rather than what is imposed upon them.

Empowerment must be at the core of personalisation. Professionals must see this emancipatory value as their focus of practice. Glasby (2009) claims that research and evidence relating to direct payments and personal budgets so far provide the most powerful tools available for increasing choice and control available to disabled people and for changing the relationship between the state and the individual. Many service users have never been given the opportunity to engage with services in this way and it is not something that will necessarily come naturally to them. It is not as simple as handing over power. It will take time and support for individuals to take the driving seat in this process and develop their skills along the way. Personalisation reinforces the idea that the individual is best placed to know what they need and how those needs can best be met. It assumes that people can be responsible and make their own decisions but people need the information and support to do so. If we return to Activity 2.5 and think about the responses of the two social workers, we can see that social worker A in the brief exchange makes assumptions about Mr Walker's abilities and wishes. She allows her own values to dominate the exchange and makes it clear that if he does choose to go against her advice, he will be doing so alone, clearly reinforcing where the power lies. In scenario B, the social worker assumes Mr Walker is capable of making a choice, she identifies that he may need more support and offers it in the form of leaflets or talking to others who have used direct payments. She makes it clear that his choice will be respected and supported and in so doing hands over power to Mr Walker, laying down the foundations for empowerment.

One final word of caution in relation to empowerment and personalisation: social workers need to guard against casual claims and assumptions that they are functioning as empowering practitioners. Empowerment instead should be viewed as an aspirational rather than attainable value or goal. Assuming we have empowered people runs the risk of an unhealthy level of complacency creeping into our practice. As individuals begin to take control of certain aspects of their life they may well begin to transfer this experience and learning to other areas of their life. When individuals make the link between the personal and political, they begin to acquire the confidence to open further opportunities to develop, liberate and transform. The role of the social worker is to ensure that information and support are offered to individuals, to carefully judge the level of support and encouragement individuals need and more importantly to know when to withdraw.

CHAPTER SUMMARY

This chapter has explored the complex relationships between those in receipt of services and those providing services. It has considered how they have emerged, and are reinforced or challenged by past, present and future government policy, ideologies, theories and models of practice. Central to the discussion is the importance of adopting anti-discriminatory and anti-oppressive practice which seeks to support service users in making connections between personal circumstances and political structures. Good partnership working based on reflective and reflexive practice provides the means to hand over control to service users in a way they feel comfortable with and confident to make meaningful changes to their lives.

Advocates of personalisation have described it as a new paradigm while the more cynical view is that it is little more than a cost-cutting exercise. In reality both perspectives have probably influenced the agenda. I would suggest that personalisation has the potential to be embraced as a new paradigm if practice is based on a comprehensive understanding of the concepts discussed in this chapter. Social care professionals need to understand why it is important to give people power before they learn how to do this. In this sense, empowering practice in personalisation is about both thinking and doing.

FURTHER READING

Duffy, S (2006) *Keys to citizenship: A guide to getting good support for people with learning disabilities* (2nd edn). Birkenhead: Paradigm.

An excellent explanation of citizenship and how it can be achieved in practice.

Glasby, J and Littlechild, R (2009) *Direct payments and personal budgets. Putting personalisation into practice* (2nd edn). Bristol: Policy Press.

This book reflects on the history of direct payment and the personalisation agenda. It refers to a range of research in relation to different service user groups and provides useful analysis throughout.

Henwood, M and Hudson, B (2007) *Here to stay? Self-directed support: Aspiration and implementation (a review for the Department of Health).* Heathencote: Melanie Henwood Associates.

A very accessible piece of research providing insight into how professionals are responding to the personalisation agenda.

Oliver, M and Sapey, B (2006) *Social work with disabled people* (3rd edn). Basingstoke: Palgrave Macmillan.

The book encourages students to critically reflect on practice and provides a good level of detail of the social model of disability both for those new to the concept and those with some grounding. The book explores the links between the social model of disability and direct payments legislation and policy and considers how far this legislation has promoted independent living principles and empowerment.

WEBSITES

www.in-control.org.uk

In Control started work in 2003 to change the social care system in England and committed to individuals being in control of their support and lives. The website has a wealth of information relating to policy, practice and experience from people directing their own support.

www.york.ac.uk/inst/spru/

Social Policy Research Unit, York University (SPRU). Their work has been concerned with the development of policies and the delivery of services to support people made vulnerable by poverty, ageing, disability or chronic illness. SPRU has an international reputation for excellence in research. There are several studies and useful articles relating to personalisation.

www.dh.gov.uk

The Department of Health has an area dedicated to personalisation and provides more details of the policies and reviews mentioned in this chapter.

Chapter 3
The social work process and role

This chapter will begin to help you meet the following National Occupational Standards.

Key role 1: Prepare for, and work with individuals, families, carers, groups and communities to assess their needs and circumstances.

* Evaluate all information to identify the best form of initial involvement.
* Inform individuals, families, carers, groups and communities about your own, and the organisation's duties and responsibilities.
* Work with individuals, families, carers, groups and communities to identify, gather, analyse and understand information.
* Work with individuals, families, carers, groups and communities to enable them to analyse, identify, clarify and express their strengths, expectations and limitations.
* Work with individuals, families and carers, groups and communities to enable them to assess and make informed decisions about their needs, circumstances, risks, preferred options and resources.
* Assess and review the preferred options of individuals, families, carers, groups and communities.
* Assess needs, risks and options taking into account legal and other requirements.

Key role 2: Plan, carry out, review and evaluate social work practice, with individuals, families, carers, groups, communities and other professionals.

* Plan and implement action to meet the immediate needs.
* Review the outcomes with individuals, families, carers, groups, communities, organisations, professionals and others.
* Apply and justify social work methods and models used to achieve change and development, and to improve life opportunities.
* Support the actions of others involved in implementing plans.
* Review the effectiveness of the plans with the people involved.

Key role 3: Support individuals to represent their needs, views and circumstances.

* Assist individuals, families, carers, groups and communities to access independent advocacy.
* Enable individuals, families, carers, groups and communities to be involved in decision-making forums.

Also important here are the General Social Care Council Codes of Practice for social care workers (GSCC, 2002), which state the following.

Social care workers must protect the rights and promote the interests of service users and carers; this includes:

* Treating each person as an individual (1.1).
* Respecting and, where appropriate, promoting the individual views and wishes of both service users and carers (1.2).
* Supporting service users' rights to control their lives and make informed choices about the services they receive (1.3).
* Respecting diversity and different cultures and values (1.6).

As a social worker, you must strive to establish and maintain trust and confidence of service users and carers. This includes:
- Being honest and trustworthy.
- Communicating in an appropriate, open, accurate and straightforward way (2.1).
- Being reliable and dependable (2.4).

As a social care worker, you must promote the independence of service users while protecting them as far as possible from danger or harm.
- Promoting the independence of service users and assisting them to understand and exercise their rights (3.1).
- Recognising and using responsibly the power that comes from your work with service users and carers (3.8).

The chapter will also introduce you to the following academic standards as set out in the 2008 social work subject benchmark statement.

5.5.1 Managing problem-solving activities.
5.5.2 Gathering information.
5.5.3 Analysis and synthesis.
5.5.4 Intervention and evaluation.
5.6 Communication skills.
5.7 Skills in working with others.

Introduction

In Chapter 1 we explored the history and meaning of personalisation and suggested that it was important to recognise that personalisation embraces four key areas: universal services; early intervention and prevention; self-directed support; and social capital. While it is important that we recognise the need to view personalisation in this broader context, it is inevitable that social workers gravitate towards self-directed support and the use of personal or individual budgets. This chapter will therefore focus on the key stages and specific social work roles involved in supporting individuals to have more choice and control in directing their own support. This will include self-assessment, support planning and reviewing.

The changes brought about as a result of personalisation and in particular the introduction of a self-directed support model have led to much debate in relation to the future role of social work. Social workers are by no means agreed on the impact personalisation will have, and while some are optimistic, others remain doubtful of any real changes to the lives of service users. On the one hand, social workers have identified personalisation as an opportunity to move away from the gatekeeping roles of care management, enabling them to engage with more traditional aspects of social work such as casework with individuals and their families. For others they sense that it will lead to increased bureaucracy and possible erosion of the social work role.

Drawing on practice examples and research findings, this chapter will explore how personalisation is being received and adopted across the country. At the time of writing there is no legislation governing this process and there are many local variations in the way personalisation is being adopted and delivered. This chapter therefore will attempt to highlight common themes and practices, providing the reader with theoretical knowledge and skills which can be adapted to individual placement and work settings.

Terminology

Before exploring the process of self-directed support, it is important to point out that there are several terms currently being used to describe services and activities within the personalisation agenda. It is worth noting that as with all new concepts, practice and terminology can evolve and change. Some of the terms are often used interchangeably and vary depending on the organisation or local authority you are working with. At this point it would be useful to take some time to study the glossary located at the back of the book.

The process

The independent charity In Control, established in 2003, was committed to finding a new way of organising social care systems. As part of its work, In Control developed a model for self-directed support. Local authorities have adopted this process in part or in full to support the implementation of self-directed support as part of the Putting People First programme of work.

While there are local variations in the way the process is used, notions of self-assessment, support planning and review are central characteristics of self-directed support. With this in mind, we will explore some of the principles and practices underpinning these key areas of the process. Understanding the subtle, yet significant, changes from traditional forms of assessment and service delivery is essential in understanding new ways of working for service users, social workers, allied professionals and care providers.

Assessment

The starting point for any adult wishing to access social care services is the NHS and Community Care Act 1990. Section 47 provides local authorities with a duty to offer an assessment to anyone who appears to have a social care need. This part of the process is carried out to make an initial assessment and up until recently *Fair access to care* (FACS) (DH, 2003c) was used to determine eligibility. This is a national eligibility framework for allocating social care resources fairly, transparently and consistently. Introduced in 2003, eligibility is divided into four categories: critical, substantial, moderate and low. The national eligibility bandings and criteria are interpreted by councils with adult social services responsibilities in respect of the needs of their community and local budgetary needs. In 2010 new government guidance relating to eligibility was published (DH, 2010a), replacing FACS (DH, 2003c). Written in light of a CSCI review, *Cutting the cake fairly* (CSCI, 2008a), it aims to set eligibility firmly within the context of both Putting People First policy (DH, 2007a) and more generally within a broader context of public services reform. Fundamentally, the guidance stresses the need to ensure that in applying eligibility criteria to prioritise individual need, local councils are not neglecting the needs of the wider population. The guidance still allows councils to operate the four categories of critical, substantial, moderate and low in addressing eligible needs but it also requires councils to consider presenting needs, which are needs that may not be as serious and may not meet the criteria but service users may benefit from some level of support. In setting criteria, therefore, local councils must consider the provision and commissioning of universal services.

In the CSCI review (2008a), it was reported that raising eligibility thresholds without putting in place adequate preventative strategies often leads to a short-term dip in the number of people eligible for social care, followed soon after by a long-term rise. The report therefore recommended that councils adopt a preventative approach to help avoid rising levels of need and cost at a later stage.

Given the current financial climate, ongoing demographic pressures of an ageing population and the government's drive for austerity, the future of setting eligibility in this way, I would suggest, remains uncertain. A survey carried out by Community Care in 2010 revealed that three-quarters of councils met critical or substantial care needs only, but this is set to rise to 80 per cent by the following year as plans to tighten thresholds by councils currently supporting moderate care needs are set in place. This represents a sharp decline in provision from 2006, when 53 per cent of councils supported moderate needs (Dunning, 2010).

Depending on the threshold of the individual local authority, there are a number of possible outcomes at this stage for the service user. It may be that a simple service, piece of equipment or one-off intervention is required. This can be picked up in the initial assessment and acted upon without requiring drawn-out assessment processes and long-term intervention. It may lead to signposting to other appropriate services, such as re-enablement, or prevention services. The initial assessment, however, may lead to the next level of assessment whereby a worker will be allocated and advice and information about the process are given to the individual.

A key change to the self-directed support process is the introduction of the notion of self-assessment whereby greater emphasis is placed on service users identifying their own needs. For many years social workers have had the power through legislation to assess the needs of vulnerable people and to manage the process of service delivery. Disabled people have argued that they should be able to assess their own needs and have the power and control over service provision (Renshaw, 2008).

ACTIVITY **3.1**

Thinking about the notion of self-assessment, make a list of the benefits and drawbacks of service users assessing their own needs.

- *What skills or expertise does the social worker have in making assessments?*

- *What skills or expertise does the service user have in making an assessment of their own needs?*

COMMENT

You may have found it relatively easy to identify the skills of the social worker. It may have been more difficult, however, to identify the expertise that the service user possesses, as it is not a word that we generally attach to a service user. It is important, however, to carefully examine our assumptions in relation to 'who is the expert?' when we work with service users.

Self-assessment

The notion of self-assessment has been a key issue since the early 1990s. Disabled activist Morris (1993a) points out that professional resistance to self-assessment based on an assumption that it would lead to insatiable demand is insulting and ignores evidence that service users are quite capable of rationing their use of services if criteria are clear. The underlying principle to self-assessment is that individuals understand their own needs better than social workers, a principle which Renshaw (2008) suggests may undermine traditional social work thinking. This concept is not new to social work and can be located within most definitions of social work, particularly when we consider social work values of respect for individuals and self-determination (BASW, 2002). Similarly, the NHS and Community Care Act 1990 reinforced the process of needs-led assessments. Community care guidance called for social workers to work in partnership with service users in agreeing needs and setting objectives to meet those needs. Care management was defined as the process of tailoring services to individual needs (DH, 1991), stressing the importance of fostering independence. Yet as Morris (2004) points out, independence is not linked to physical or intellectual capacity to care for oneself without assistance but it is about having control over that support and when and how that assistance is provided. This definition of independence remains centrally important in our understanding of self-directed support.

Person-centred planning

In order to ensure the service user is placed at the centre of each stage of the process from assessment through to support planning and finally to review, social workers must adopt a person-centred approach to their work. As discussed in Chapter 1, person-centred planning approaches seek to use what is important to the individual as the focus for developing support and change. This model of practice has been adopted as a key method for delivering the personalisation objectives in the Putting People First programme for social care (DH, 2008b).

The person-centred approach is very much reflected in the self-directed model of assessment developed by In Control, whereby service users are encouraged to be centrally involved in this process from the start rather than it being a professionally driven document which at best might be shared with the service user on completion.

It is important that we see assessment as a shared process in which the service user has the skills and expertise to fully engage in the process. The skill of the social worker is to help draw out that expertise so service users can confidently express their own needs. Many people using services have been historically disempowered by dependency-creating welfare services and often lack the confidence and knowledge to identify their needs or to make informed choices about the support they need (Priestley, 2004). Furthermore, they may not have the professional language to express their needs in ways which match proc-ess-driven forms. It is important that the social worker acknowledges this and supports service users to identify their own needs. At a strategic level it is important to develop inclusive mechanisms and paperwork which enable service users to articulate their needs in a way which makes sense to themselves rather than the wider organisation. It is also important to note the added value that independent organisations such as Centres of Independent/Integrated Living (CILs) can offer in supporting service users in the self-assessment process (Renshaw, 2008).

Self-assessment questionnaire

Most local authorities now use some form of a self-assessment questionnaire which the service user works through either alone or with a professional. Most questionnaires ask service users to score their needs against each question. At the end the points are added up and an overall score is given. The questionnaire asks a number of questions based on several domains covering all aspects of social care, including for example:

• personal care needs;

• nutritional needs;

• practical/daily living;

• physical and mental well-being;

• relationships and social inclusion;

• choice and control;

• risk;

• family carer and social support.

Assessment details

The depth and detail of the assessment should be proportionate to an individual's needs, enabling more resources to be focused on those with complex needs. Social workers must recognise that individuals may perceive different hierarchies of need and may focus on seemingly low-level needs as being more important to them than those that may appear more obvious and serious in terms of health, well-being and risk from a professional perspective. While it is important that social workers remain mindful and watchful of risk or potential risk, it is equally important in a self-assessment process to allow the service user to direct the process at the pace and sequence that he or she is comfortable with. This may be challenging to social workers who have traditionally worked within a more prescribed framework such as care management where the professional lead and judgement are central to the process.

CASE STUDY

Mr Shah has returned home after a four-week stay in hospital following a broken hip. In assessing his own needs, among other requirements he requests for help to put his tie on. The social worker initially brushes over this comment given the high level of personal care Mr Shah will need in the coming weeks. Mr Shah becomes quite frustrated and impatient. He is soon unable to focus on other aspects of his support needs and repeats his request for help with his tie. The social worker eventually acknowledges how important this is to

Continued

Mr Shah. She moves the discussion to the tie and Mr Shah explains that he has always worn a tie and feels uncomfortable without one when meeting people outside the family. The social worker ensures that this is recorded and reassures Mr Shah that this will be included as part of a support plan. Mr Shah is then able to identify and discuss more serious personal and health care needs.

- *Why might the social worker have missed the initial request?*

- *How could a person-centred approach have helped in this situation?*

COMMENT

The social worker clearly missed the issue of the tie as she was focused on some of the serious social and health care needs. By adopting a person-centred approach which encourages Mr Shah to take a lead in the process and uses his perspective as a starting point, the relationship and trust are likely to develop at a quicker and more meaningful pace. Valuing and responding to Mr Shah's needs in this way provides a good foundation for facilitating a self-directed model of support.

Within the assessment process it is important that the social worker encourages and enables people to make the best use of their own strengths, capabilities and resources to live independently. Thompson (2005) reminds social workers of the importance of focusing on strengths and avoiding the tendency to see themselves as problem-solvers who concentrate solely on weaknesses and see their role as fixing situations and providing expert advice. Thompson (2005, p. 82), warns against social workers creating a *pseudo-medical* relationship with service users where the social worker is the expert who diagnoses the problem and prescribes the cure. In Chapter 5 service user Eric, in his narrative, describes this approach happening to him and how it prevented him from taking control of his support and life in a positive way.

Developments in the self-assessment process and the self-directed model of support in general have raised a number of questions in relation to the future role for social workers in this process. In Chapter 7, we will explore some of the specific roles for the social worker in relation to the self-directed support process, but generally some of the ways social workers can support service users include the following.

- Supporting service users and carers to identify and articulate their own needs both verbally and through written forms.

- Supporting people through major transitions often involving loss. Assessments often take place at times of stress where individuals are adjusting to major transitions such as the loss of a loved one or a new illness or disability.

- Supporting service users to negotiate with members of their family or friends who may all have different perceptions, values, expectations or needs.

Clearly the tasks and roles mentioned above require specific expertise and skills which it could be argued lie at the heart of social work practice. As mentioned above, the introduction of self-assessment has raised questions about the need for social work input if service users are doing it for themselves. Key skills are required to facilitate service users to identify and articulate their own needs while supporting often fragile, sensitive and difficult situations and relationships in order to sustain long-term positive outcomes.

One of the common misconceptions of self-assessment is that it is a process that is exclusive to the service user. The aim of self-assessment, however, is that service users fully participate in the process based on the principle that they are most likely to be the best experts on themselves. The expertise of the professional is therefore to advise, support and facilitate the service user through this process, contributing their own expertise and experience in relation to the process. In Chapter 2, we examined the power relations that exist between service users and social workers and acknowledged the need for social workers to develop anti-discriminatory ways of working which seek to reduce power differentials, leading to emancipatory practice. In this way, self-assessment requires workers to redefine their expertise and professional role but does not assume they are no longer needed.

In some cases there may be discrepancies between how the service user and the professional perceive their needs. This can be very difficult for the service user, who may feel disempowered and struggles to assert his or her views in a professional manner. Social workers need to be skilled in asking challenging questions in a sensitive manner which acknowledges the power imbalance between professional and service user. Practitioners need to help identify when conflicts are likely to occur and support service users to access independent support or advocacy where appropriate and possible to ensure the assessment remains as objective as possible and service users have a voice in the process.

There are times when the professional assessment and the service user assessment have to be referred to the next level of management within an organisation. This might be because of different perceptions in the level of need or issues of risk identified by the social worker. This can really test the social worker's ability to work within the principles of self-directed support. Good practice does not require social workers to collude with service users and permit unsafe activities or support. It does, however, require them to work within a framework which respects service users, enabling them to retain as much control and direction over their support as is possible, as demonstrated in the following case study.

CASE STUDY

Eamonn is a 24-year-old man with learning and physical disabilities. He has lived at home with his older brother for the last ten years since his parents died. Eamonn now wants to live alone and has completed a self-assessment form in which he has indicated that his needs are minimal. The social worker has met Eamonn on a number of occasions and spent time with his brother. Both the social worker and Eamonn's brother agree that Eamonn has a much higher level of need than he has highlighted in the self-assessment questionnaire.

Continued

The social worker is also aware that Eamonn has full capacity to make life choices so she has to deal sensitively with Eamonn in supporting him through this process. The social worker suggests that Eamonn accesses support from a local advocacy project.

Eamonn agrees to this support and after spending time with a citizen advocate starts to recognise and accept that he may have more complex needs than he first indicated. At a planning meeting Eamonn is supported by his advocate to explain his wish to live as independently as possible. Eamonn explains that he doesn't want lots of different people supporting him and that he wants more time on his own but accepts that he may need to accept more support than he ideally would wish.

In recognising the dilemma for Eamonn the social worker assures him that a creative support plan with the possible use of assistive technologies might avoid him having to have a lot of support hours. She also discusses the option for Eamonn to be fully involved in recruiting any support workers.

COMMENT

In the case study above the social worker has challenged the self-assessment made by Eamonn in a sensitive manner. Through accessing independent support, she has given him time and space to reflect on his assessment. She has enabled him to express his concerns in the meeting with the help of an advocate and she has taken his views on board. Although she has challenged his assessment, she has also remained true to the principles of self-directed support by enabling him to maximise his control and direction over the support he does receive. Social work often requires balancing choice versus risk. This is a complex process when working with adults who have full capacity to make decisions. We will explore this issue in more detail in Chapter 6.

ACTIVITY *3.2*

There are many variations in the way each local authority organises the assessment process. Look at a couple of local authority websites and search for information relating to self-directed support. Most local authorities will have a web page dedicated to self-directed support.

For example, search 'Lancashire self-directed support'.

Compare the similarities and differences in the way each local authority undertakes the process. You will find that most are based to at least some degree on the original model provided by In Control in 2003.

You may have spotted some key differences in the format or the content of the assessment process. The service user, however, should always be located at the centre of this process. You may have found a local authority which allows or encourages service users to take complete control of this process and may also leave space for them to describe their own needs in their own words without the restrictions of formatted questions. Others are more prescriptive and will insist that the assessment process is a professionally supported process. These are interesting differences as they can tell us a lot about the principles and politics underlying the organisation.

Resource allocation

You may have come across the acronym RAS, which stands for 'resource allocation system'. Once the assessment has been completed, the local authority needs to decide how much money a person is entitled to for them to stay healthy and safe. A number of local authorities have adopted the resource allocation system to enable this process to happen. The system was developed by In Control in 2003 and continues to be refined by In Control and local authorities who adapt it to their own systems and structures.

In short, the resource allocation system is simply a framework to understand and describe needs and provide a methodology for the conversion of needs to money. The self-assessment questionnaire leads to a number of points and the points are then converted into an amount of money which is referred to as the 'indicative amount' or the 'indicative allocation'. At the time of writing there is no national RAS or requirement for one but each local authority will have developed some means of working out how to convert needs into a sum of money. In 2009, Adult Directors of Social Services (ADASS) in association with In Control produced a *Common Resource Allocation Framework* (ADASS, 2009) with the aim of addressing some of the technical, financial, legal and policy difficulties local authorities were experiencing in administering the current RAS system. It is hoped the *Common Resource Allocation Framework* will enable a more standardised approach in which everyone with similar needs and circumstances is treated equitably.

Financial assessment and contribution

Once an indicative amount has been identified, the council will assess the service user's financial circumstances in accordance with the guidance on *Fairer charging* (DH, 2003c). The council will then work out what the service user's maximum contribution will be in accordance with *Fairer contribution* guidance (DH, 2010b).

Support planning

The support plan is the means by which information is presented to a local council in order to agree the release of funds as an individual or personal budget. The support plan highlights the lifestyle choices and wishes of the individual and demonstrates how the individual intends to spend the money to meet their aims.

The support plan must be outcome-focused and should reflect the needs identified in the self-assessment. The outcomes should be specific and indicate how they will improve the health and well-being of the individual and will keep them safe. A good support plan will also highlight any personal outcomes, which are things the person wants to achieve or change in life, as a direct result of being able to get the support that they need.

The support planning process begins once the funds available have been agreed through the RAS process. At this point the social worker will make the service user aware of the funds available and will discuss the support planning process. It is important for the social worker to provide information about what support planning entails and who might be able to help them with it. We will explore both of these issues in further detail below. The key social work role is to enable planning to happen. For some individuals this support may be minimal. It may, for example, involve providing basic information and signposting individuals to useful resources. For others it may involve more intensive support. (Duffy, 2010) suggests that social work support should be focused on developing personalised support for the minority of people where no one else can provide the significant help they need. Duffy continues to reinforce the importance of equipping people to plan for themselves and to be in control. He suggests that social workers need to know how and when to intervene in the planning and implementation process and that this is central to good social work practice. The ability to know when and how to offer an indirect and facilitative approach which is more likely to have longer-term benefits and avoids creating dependency or a sense of incompetence from the service user's perspective can be a challenging task for the social worker.

It is important to acknowledge that support planning is not a one-off activity and that individuals are supported to continue to update and refine their support plan. This is important for two reasons. First, the support plan may need to be updated as individuals achieve outcomes or wish to change the outcome or support they receive. Secondly, ongoing support planning is particularly important for someone with fluctuating or rapidly changing conditions that may impact on their capacity to consent. In such cases there may be a need to continually refine the support plan to ensure that it meets their own priorities, needs and goals while ensuring they are safe and it is having a positive impact on their health and well-being.

For people who do lack the capacity to consent, it is important to ensure the support plan focuses on decision-making. In some cases it may be appropriate to set supported decision-making principles and agreements. Following the Mental Capacity Act 2005 Code of Practice, good practice in supported decision-making allows individuals to be supported to provide capacity to consent (DH, 2008c).

Support plans should be developed in a way that addresses risks in a proportionate and flexible manner. Clearly, it is important to ensure that the support plan explores issues of risk or potential risk and puts into place agreed safeguards. For some individuals, however, safeguarding mechanisms will not be necessary or appropriate and it is important that organisations and practitioners avoid employing a standardised procedure or universal form that has to be completed for each individual. Some local authorities have introduced additional documents relating specifically to what could go wrong and how a person may manage that. This document can then be adopted as an integral part of the support planning process.

The support plan

The support plan needs to address some key areas for them to be signed off by the local council and to release the funds. In Control has developed the following seven criteria which should be addressed in order for this to happen. Many local councils have adopted or adapted this model in establishing local support planning processes.

1. What is important to you?

2. What do you want to change or achieve?

3. How will you spend the money?

4. How will you use your individual budget?

5. How will your support be managed?

6. How will you stay in control of your life?

7. What are you going to do to make this plan happen?
    (In Control, 2007)

The local council will need to be satisfied that all the above questions have been addressed and that issues of risk have been considered and safeguards put in place where necessary in order to agree the release of the funds.

As with the self-assessment, the service user can choose how they will develop their support plan. They may decide to do it in one or more of the following ways.

- *On their own* Some service users may choose to complete their support plan without any support. It is important to recognise the strengths and resources some service users have in accessing and organising support. The advent of the internet and other technologies has enabled many service users to research and secure support and services which are specifically suited to helping them achieve outcomes (see the case study below).

- *Help from family or friends* Service users can organise themselves into a trust called a 'trust circle'. This is a legal entity and can be very helpful to people who need support in making decisions or need others to do so on their behalf.

- *Service providers* Service users may already have a good relationship with a service provider who knows a lot about them. The service user may wish to ask them to help develop the support plan.

- *Person-centred facilitator*.

- *Care manager or social worker* It is important that social workers see support planning as part of their role, providing this is the choice of the service user. In the past the initial assessment often dominated practice, sometimes paying less attention to other stages of the process such as care planning and reviewing. Glasby (2009) suggests that the self-directed support model has reversed the current practice and a focus on the support planning stage is a better place to start in ensuring the best possible support arrangements are put in place. In Chapter 7, we will explore some of the specific social work roles and skills in relation to support planning.

- *Independent people or organisations* Some service users may choose to access support from someone outside their council. It is likely that the service user will have to pay for this support but they can include this as part of the support plan. They may use different individuals or agencies to help them with different aspects of their plan. For example, they may use a life coach to help them think about changes, a technician to advise them on assistive technologies and a financial adviser to help them work out the best use of the budget. Some of the independent agents may include: centres of independent living; support brokers; independent advocates; direct payment support schemes; independent person-centred planning facilitators; life coaches; financial advisers.

CASE STUDY

Jack worked for many years in computer programming until he had to retire on health grounds due to a motorcycle accident. As a result Jack has significant mobility difficulties and he needs support with aspects of his personal care and daily living. Jack is very independent and wants to minimise the number of personal assistants that come into his home. Through his knowledge and skill in computing, he has managed to source and manage various devices or systems that have allowed him to remain as independent as possible. In his support plan, Jack identified several devices, including a speech recognition and screen reader system which allows him hands-free control of his PC. He has also spent time researching and sourcing the most effective and cost-efficient devices to allow him to stay alone at night. Among other things he has bought a bed occupancy sensor which sends an alert if he has been out of bed for longer than a certain time that he can set. If Jack gets up in the night there is a risk that he may fall and be unable to get back to bed. The device sets an alarm which links to the mobile phone of his personal assistant, who will then come to the house and support him. The same sensor also switches on a lamp which helps him in the dark if he has fallen. The cost of this device and the cost of the personal assistant who is on call are much less than paying for someone to stay the night and as Jack believes, it has enabled him to remain at home.

Jack is now using his knowledge and skills to advise others wanting similar devices and hopes to set up a business in the near future.

It is important that you understand the differences between the self-directed model of support and care management. Once you have researched the two approaches you may even wish to question the degree to which there is a difference in the two models. Care management was formally introduced with the NHS and Community Care Act 1990 and implemented in 1993. It was described as the cornerstone of high-quality care (DH, 1989) and advocated care management as an effective method of targeting resources and planning services to meet specific needs of individual clients. The paper described care management as being responsive and able to adapt services to individual needs and the rationale for this refocusing and targeted approach was the empowerment of users and carers. It insisted that service users and carers would be able to exercise the same power as consumers of other services and that redressing the balance of power in this way would offer the best guarantee of a continuing improvement of the quality of the service.

It could be argued that much of the language and principles referred to above could be used to describe a self-directed model of support; so what are, if any, the key differences in the two models?

Look at the two processes below and make some notes about the similarities and differences between the two approaches.

Care management model	**Self-directed model**
Assessment of need	Self-assessment
Care planning	RAS
Implementing the care plan	Support planning
Monitor	Implementing the support plan
Review	Review

COMMENT

You might have assumed that there was in fact little difference between the models. Both models include an assessment, a process of identifying and arranging support and services and reviewing the support once it is in place. As suggested above, there is much shared language in these two approaches which appear to be rooted within self-deterministic principles. However, if we look a little deeper at some of the language used to describe the tasks we can start to identify some of the subtle, yet significant, differences.

As discussed in Chapter 2, one of the key levers for individuals gaining more control of their support came with the introduction of direct payments. The freedom and flexibility that came along with having money in their own hands cannot be overestimated, both in terms of personal spending power but perhaps more importantly the small victory it represented for disabled people who campaigned for many years for the right to control their own support in this way. The release of funds to the individual is certainly one of the most, if not the most, striking difference between these two models.

Person-centred planning (PCP)

As stated earlier in the chapter, PCP has been adopted as a key method for delivering the personalisation objectives. PCP shares many of its values with those underlying the support planning process, including respect, choice, ownership, opportunity and support (Sanderson, 2000). Within a self-directed support model, there is an expectation that service users' strengths and gifts are acknowledged, highlighted, respected and capitalised upon. In the same way the notion of choice is placed at the centre of the support planning process and the key word, 'support', is perceived to be the valued role of professionals involved in the process. Support in this sense is different from leading, chairing, managing or co-ordinating, all of which are terms often attached to a professional. Finally the shared value, ownership, signifies the importance of adopting a PCP approach within support planning. Ownership implies that it is more than being supported to make choices and decisions but means the individual has the final and total authority in their own life (Sanderson, 2000). It will be useful to refer to the websites noted at the end of the chapter, where you will find more information and example support plans that have adopted person-centred thinking and practice within their approach.

ACTIVITY **3.4**

Now that you have read about support planning, this activity will give you an opportunity to put it into practice. Case studies in relation to personalisation are very useful as they help you to reflect on the creative ways people have organised their support. This activity will help you think more creatively about support and enable you to help service users to think 'outside the box'.

> **You are the lucky winner of £1,000.**
>
> Your local council has awarded you with the above money to spend as you choose to improve your health and well-being.
>
> Here are the rules:
>
> 1. You must spend it all within a year.
>
> 2. You cannot spend it on anything illegal or to pay off any debts.
>
> 3. You cannot give it away.
>
> 4. You must demonstrate the outcomes you will achieve for all the money i.e. how will it improve your *health and well-being*?
>
> Use the box below to complete this task
>
> Your local council will confirm whether or not your application has been successful.

Complete the box below.

Amount £	Item/activity	Outcome – how will it improve your health and well-being?

Continued

You may have found it relatively easy to think about how you would spend this money; but did you find it as simple to provide outcomes which would improve your health and well-being? If you compare your own box with others in your group, you will note the diverse ways in which people spent their money. We all have different priorities along with different responsibilities and networks of support. The importance of this activity is to demonstrate how diverse individuals are in identifying needs and wishes. If you had all been given a year's membership at a gym which you could only attend on Monday mornings, would this have suited the whole group? I hope you and the other students in the group employed some creative thinking. Some of the examples other students have provided me with in the classroom include: speed dating; buying a tipi; meditation course at a Buddhist centre; riding lessons; driving lessons; cookery course; and buying a set of pans.

Support brokerage

Embedded in any discussion about personalisation are frequent references to the notion of brokerage. Although it is generally accepted that self-directed support relies upon adequate support brokerage, it is less clear what is meant by brokerage, where it should sit and who should do it. The journal article highlighted in the Further Reading at the end of the chapter will give you a fuller appreciation of this discourse but the information that follows will give you a flavour of some of the emerging debates.

Think of a time when you have a used a broker. It might have been to book a holiday, arrange a mortgage, or set up a rental agreement.

- *What did the broker do for you?*

- *Why did you need them?*

- *How did you find them and choose them?*

- *Could you have done it another way?*

- *Do you have any friends or family who could have helped you with all or any part of the example arrangement?*

You may have used a broker because you lacked knowledge or expertise in an area. You may have used the broker to help you get the best deal, to get an independent view, or maybe you felt you had no other choice. You may have used a broker to save you time or because you needed something very quickly. You may have spoken to family or friends with prior knowledge. For example, you might have asked for ideas about a holiday or compared mortgage options. You may have used the internet or literature to help you develop your knowledge and expertise in a certain area. All of these are ways of using brokerage and in many ways are similar to support brokerage, as we will see.

A 'broker' (noun) is described as *a person who buys or sells goods or assets for others.* The verb means *to arrange or negotiate (a deal or plan)* (Oxford English Dictionary, 2005). There is some suggestion that the term 'brokerage' was used within the context of care management (Payne, 1995) but it has really come to prominence in the context of the personalisation agenda and self-directed support.

Much of the literature and government guidance avoids describing support brokerage as a specific role but commonly uses the term to describe a range of features and functions to help individuals arrange and manage their support. In this sense support brokerage is said to include the following key functions.

- To find out what is available.

- To explore what is possible.

- To provide information.

- To give technical advice.

- To encourage and develop informal support.

- To co-ordinate support and resources.

- To assist the person to manage their obligation and responsibilities in relation to the budget.

- Facilitation to enable things to happen.

- Help with support planning.

(DH, 2008c)

Typically individuals use support brokers to support them in the assessment and support planning phases of the self-directed support process. It might involve help to complete the self-assessment or to design and manage the support plan.

There is no single model of support brokerage and as with your own example, service users have options in relation to accessing the type of brokerage they prefer. RIPRA (2008) describes a range of models of support brokerage including: independent brokers; independent advocacy agencies; service providers; local authorities where care managers carry out support brokerage; families or friends; or a mix of any of these. The key debates in relation to support brokerage and social work centre on whether it should be an independent role located outside of the statutory sector and whether support brokerage is part of the social work role. Scourfield (2010, p. 859) suggests that:

> *where brokerage is situated organisationally and ideologically is not inconsequential both in terms of accountability, profile and quality of the brokers and the extent to which service users can feel properly in control of their own care and support.*

The debate in relation to whether brokerage should be part of the social work role is complex and unresolved. Some social workers are resistant to being seen purely as a broker and there is also a concern about releasing the role to the independent sector. On the one hand, the opportunity for service users to access independent support outside the assessment process is welcomed but a potential lack of regulation and professionalism makes others cautious of this role being transferred (Scourfield, 2010). Furthermore, there is a fear that the current need to ration services and jobs will provide the government with a convenient means of scaling down the social work role in relation to adults. Aware of scarce resources, social workers are quite right in questioning the future of social work and how it will position itself in relation to support brokerage. At this stage it is unclear as to whether the two can co-exist or whether in fact support brokerage is a direct threat to not only social work jobs but the profession as a whole. While there remains uncertainty and confusion in the role and location of brokerage, it would seem clear that brokerage is now considered a critical element for service users in accessing and managing their support. It will, however, be important to resolve these debates and avoid assuming that the creation of a new term such as support brokerage with its current vagueness will succeed. As Scourfield (2010, p. 864) suggests, *it allows policy makers to suggest that great transformations (e.g. people power) are just around the corner, without spelling out exactly how they will take place.*

RESEARCH SUMMARY

In response to the personalisation agenda, the GSCC, SCIE and other partner agencies have examined social work tasks and roles and concluded that social work skills were critical to achieving the ambitions of the personalisation agenda.

In 2008, the GSCC provided a statement of social work roles and tasks for the twenty-first century. In particular, it recognised links between the core principles of social work and personalisation including:

- *a preventative approach;*

- *the ability to work with complex situations and with different agencies and sectors;*

- *the capacity to perform a wide range of tasks including brokerage and advocacy;*

- *flexibility to step outside agency boundaries to serve people's best interests yet with the security of working in a regulated profession within a framework of law and regulation where people are accountable for their practice (GSCC, 2008).*

The GSCC states that social workers should be applying and extending the principles of personalisation, which have always been at the heart of social work at its best, to help people find individual solutions and achieve satisfactory outcomes *(GSCC, 2008, page 15).*

RESEARCH SUMMARY

Empirical research was undertaken by David and Janet Leece in 2010 to explore the perceptions of 66 disabled people, carers and older people in relation to the role social workers should perform in a personalised world. Using a grounded-theory approach, obtaining data from a thread posted on 18 internet forums, the research revealed that notions of power of social workers and statutory organisations were of key concern to the

Continued

respondents. One strand of the research explored the role of brokerage and whether this can and should be a social work function.

It will be useful to spend more time reading the paper, but some of the interesting findings in relation to support brokerage are noted below.

Respondents were overwhelmingly in favour of brokers who are independent from social services, as the following quotations indicate.

> I don't think it is appropriate for social workers to become support brokers – at least not the social workers who are employed by the local authority. Having an in house service makes it all too easy for conflicts to occur whether that be financial conflicts or when it comes to risk enablement.

> An advocate independent of the local authority is a good idea in my opinion … social workers are bound by rules and regulations as to how much they can actually help.

The researchers suggest that the comments above reflect a perceived concept of institutional power. In the paper, Leece and Leece (2010) assert that choosing and employing their own support workers can enable disabled people to have greater control over their support and that by stating their preference for independent brokers, respondents were expressing their desire to avoid institutional power and the impact it has over their lives.

Review

The review phase of the self-directed model provides an opportunity for the service user to reflect on his or her support plan. It is important that the principles of choice, flexibility and self-determination are fully embraced during the reviewing phase. Focusing on the strengths and expertise of the service user, it is the social worker's role to support individuals to reflect on and review the outcomes that have been set as part of their support plan. Many councils have adopted the term 'outcome focused' to describe this process. This term describes a process that puts the main focus on the results being achieved for the person and his or her family. The outcomes identified in the support plan enable the service user and the social worker to determine how well the support plan is working. In this sense it allows for a methodical process for the social worker to record progress against a set of projected outcomes or targets.

The service user should be encouraged to review both the practical outcomes and the personal outcomes. The starting point of support planning focuses on two key questions.

1. What is important to me?

2. What do I want to change?

It is therefore important that the review considers whether the things that are important to the person have been realised and whether this has led to any change. This person-centred approach asserts that if we focus on what people want as well as what they need, overall success is more likely (Sanderson 2000).

Clearly, the social worker has a role to play in reviewing how money has been spent and the impact this has had on the person's health and well-being. The role also involves reviewing the brokerage arrangements and providing support if there are any difficulties or dissatisfaction in this area. It is important that the social worker recognises the complexity of arrangements and relationships for individuals using a number of independent agencies and organisations. Duffy (2010) suggests that the reviewing stage offers the best opportunity to help people make improvements to their lives. He states that once people have had a chance to control their budget, they are in a better position to review what is working and ways things can be improved.

At the review it is the social worker's role to ensure the service user is remaining in control of their support. To do this, social workers need to adopt an anti-discriminatory approach in their one-to-one work with the service user. They also need to demonstrate an awareness of the wider structural issues of power and oppression which impact on service users dependent on others for their support. This requires the adoption of an anti-oppressive approach, which Braye (2001) describes as one in which they are willing to question and challenge situations in a bid to bring about fundamental changes in power.

CHAPTER SUMMARY

In this chapter we have explored the social work roles and tasks involved in the self-directed model of support. We have reflected on the ideological, political and practical similarities and differences between care management and the self-directed model of support. The chapter has provided an overview of the common frameworks and mechanisms used by councils to support service users in this way, including the way budgets are allocated to service users and the process of support brokerage which seeks to support individuals in choosing, arranging and managing their support. At the same time the chapter highlighted the local variations in the way this process is managed. Qualifying students will be able to use this information to prepare for practice and consider some of the important questions and potential opportunities and challenges they may face once in practice. Qualified practitioners working in this field will be able to reflect on this chapter in relation to their own organisational processes and individual practice in considering whether and in what ways this agenda has changed the lives of service users and their own social work tasks and roles.

The chapter fully acknowledges the ambiguity, uncertainty, confusion and divergence of views that surround the self-directed model both in terms of its perceived legitimacy and value as well as the practicalities including understanding of the new social work role. Findings from a survey carried out by Community Care in 2008 suggested that social workers are divided equally on whether they believe the personalisation agenda is the right direction for social care. The findings, however, also show profound suspicion among the workforce in terms of what is meant by personalisation, with only a minority of those interviewed feeling well informed about self-directed support (Ahmed, 2008). Finally, the current economical and political context will influence both the perceptions and reality in relation to future social work roles and the personalisation agenda.

FURTHER READING

Renshaw, C (2008) Do self-assessment and self-directed support undermine traditional social work with disabled people? *Disability and Society*, 23 (3): 283–6.

The article considers the changes self-assessment will bring to the social work role and explores the impact this may have on power dynamics between service users and professionals.

Scourfield, P (2010) Going for brokerage: A task of independent support or social work? *British Journal of Social Work*, 40 (3), April 2010.

This article explores the emergence of this new language of brokerage. It considers the various ideas in relation to what brokerage is and who is supposed to undertake it.

The Department of Health has produced a series of practical guides supporting the process of self-directed support as part of the wider framework of Putting People First: Transforming Adult Social Care services. It is worth spending some time looking at the following two guides to develop your understanding of this process. Both the following guides have some excellent examples and templates of support planning and outcome-focused reviews.

DH (2008c) *Good practice in support planning and brokerage: Putting people first personalisation toolkit*. London: DH.

DH (2009) *Outcome focused reviews. A practical guide. Part of the putting people first*. Transforming adult social care services series. London: DH.

WEBSITES

Much of the information relating to the process of self-directed support is located on government and independent organisations' websites. It will be useful to research the websites below where you will find discussion and examples of self-assessment, support planning, support brokerage and reviewing.

www.centreforwelfarereform.org

This website contains a number of useful articles related to personalisation. One of the functions of the Centre for Welfare Reform is to publish information, ideas and innovations so that citizens, families and communities can improve their own lives or begin to reform those parts of the welfare systems in which they are involved.

www.helensandersonassociates.co.uk/

Helen Sanderson Associates is an international development, training and consultancy team. The organisation works with people to change their lives, organisations and communities through person-centred thinking and planning.

www.in-control.org.uk

This website provides a range of material relating to the philosophy, policy and practice of self-directed support. There are lots of examples of individuals directing their own support.

www.supportplanning.org/

This website provides information, articles and examples of support planning. It is linked to work carried out by In Control and Helen Sanderson Associates.

www.scie.org.uk

The Social Care Institute for Excellence website will keep you informed of up-to-date developments related to personalisation. There is an e-learning resource and Social Care TV clips, which will support your learning around self-directed support and personalisation.

Chapter 4
Service user groups and personalisation

ACHIEVING A SOCIAL WORK DEGREE

This chapter will begin to help you to meet the following National Occupational Standards.

Key role 1: Prepare for, and work with individuals, families, carers, groups and communities to assess their needs and circumstances.
- Work with individuals, families, carers, groups and communities to enable them to analyse, identify, clarify and express their strengths, expectations and limitations.
- Work with individuals, families, carers, groups and communities to enable them to assess and make informed decisions about their needs, circumstances, risks, preferred options and resources.

Key role 2: Plan, carry out, review and evaluate social work practice, with individuals, families, carers, groups, communities, and other professionals.
- Interact with individuals, families, carers, groups and communities to achieve change and development and to improve life opportunities.
- Examine with individuals, families, carers, groups, communities and others, support networks which can be accessed and developed.

Key role 3: Support individuals to represent their needs, views and circumstances.
- Advocate with, and on behalf of, individuals, families, carers, groups and communities.
- Assist individuals, families, carers, groups and communities to access independent advocacy.

This chapter will also refer to the General Social Care Council Codes of Practice for social care workers (GSCC, 2002), which state the following.

As a social care worker, you must protect the rights and promote the interests of service users and carers.
- Treating each person as an individual (1.1).
- Respecting, and where appropriate, promoting the individual views and wishes of both service users and carers (1.2).
- Supporting service users' rights to control their lives and make informed choices about the services they receive (1.3).
- Respecting diversity and different cultures and values (1.6).

As a social care worker, you must promote the independence of service users while protecting them as far as possible from danger or harm.
- Recognising and using responsibly the power that comes from your work with service users and carers (3.8).

As a social care worker you must respect the rights of service users while seeking to ensure that their behaviour does not harm themselves or other people.
- Recognising that service users have the right to take risks and helping them to identify and manage potential and actual risks to themselves and others (4.1).

This chapter will also introduce you to the following academic standards as set out in the 2008 social work subject benchmark statement.

5.5.3 Analysis and synthesis.
5.6 Communication skills.
5.7 Skills in working with others.

Introduction

This chapter will explore the experience of personalisation and self-directed support from the perspective of the different service user groups. There are now more than 30,000 people in England with personal budgets, which represents a massive increase since 2003, when a total of 60 people in six pilot projects were receiving personal budgets (Tyson et al., 2010). Throughout this chapter I will be referring to several evaluations that have been carried out since 2003, including reports from In Control, at three stages of their pilot projects (Poll et al., 2006; Hatton et al., 2008; Tyson et al., 2010), and the national evaluation of individual budgets carried out by the Department of Health, frequently referred to as the Ibsen study (Glendinning et al., 2008). These evaluations are sources of valuable information relating to service users' experiences of personal budgets and self-directed support, although it is argued that there are different terms of reference among these different evaluations. While the In Control evaluations aim to evaluate the experiences of self-directed support, the Ibsen study also endeavours to evaluate the integration of different funding streams with social care budgets, leading to a more complex picture (Glasby and Littlechild, 2009). The data, therefore, from all of these evaluations requires careful and considered scrutiny. As with any evaluative research, it is important to be aware of the underpinning ideology informing the research. Also, to recognise the potential for bias within self-selected pilots – local authorities may volunteer to participate in a pilot project for a variety of pragmatic and economic reasons, in addition to aspirations to improve their service provision. Additionally, service users may come forward because they are particularly disenchanted with current provision, and therefore they may have an intrinsic motivation to make self-directed support work (Glasby and Littlechild, 2009).

At this stage it is useful to consider the background to these evaluations in some more detail before examining the findings in relation to the specific service user groups.

The Ibsen study

As this is such an influential piece of evaluation, it is worth spending time to familiarise yourself with the background to, and details of, the data. While I am providing a summary here, it is important that you also consult the full report, available at www.york.ac.uk/spru from where the following information has been taken.

In 2005, 13 local authorities piloted the use of individual budgets, with outcome evaluations at six months, and a further follow-up evaluation at two years. The remit of the pilot included that service users in the individual budget sample were to have a greater input into the assessment of their needs. They were to be encouraged to identify the outcomes they wanted to achieve, and the ways in which they wanted to achieve these outcomes. Individuals would know from the initial stages the actual amount of money available for them to use, rather than finding this out at the end of an assessment process, and the emphasis was on individuals using their budgets to purchase a wide range of services, possibly including existing social care services, but also including community or commercial services.

The pilot sites were each given an additional £350,000–£400,000 over the two years, to support the initial implementation of individual budgets, but the rest of the financial resources required had to come from existing social care budgets. Sites were asked to try to integrate resources from other funding streams also, so that an individual budget could potentially be made up of resources from Access to Work, the Independent Living Fund, Supporting People and the Disabled Facilities Grant and Integrated Community Equipment Services – in addition to resources from social care budgets.

A total of 959 service users participated, across the 13 pilot sites. These participants were divided into two groups, with 510 service users receiving individual budgets, and 449 service users receiving traditional service provision, thus forming the comparison group. A number of assessment tools were employed to measure outcomes. The General Health Questionnaire (GHQ) was used to measure psychological well-being. The Adult Social Care Outcome Toolkit (ASCOT) measured social care domains ranging from personal care to social participation. Outcomes were measured in terms of:

• overall satisfaction with the support planning process and financial arrangements;

• aspirations of people accepting the offer of an individual budget;

• quality of life, well-being and unmet needs;

• ASCOT domains – personal care/comfort, control, meals, safety, accommodation, occupation, social participation.

In Control

In Control is a national programme which aims to change the organisation of social care in England so that people who use support can take more control of their lives (NIMHE, 2006). Throughout this chapter, the findings from the Ibsen study will be considered alongside the findings from the evaluations conducted by In Control (Poll et al., 2006; Hatton et al., 2008; Tyson et al., 2010). While the evaluation of In Control's first phase, 2003–2005, was based on a small sample of 31 people with learning disabilities to assess the impact of self-directed support on their lives, the findings indicated that self-directed support had the potential to promote choice and control, and satisfaction with support received (Poll et al., 2006). The evaluation of the second phase, 2005–2007, involved a larger sample of 196 service users with personal budgets across 17 local authorities in England. Within this sample group, 58 per cent had learning difficulties, 20 per cent had physical disabilities, and older people represented the remaining 13 per cent of the sample (Hatton et al., 2008). Again there were encouraging findings, with participants reporting either positive changes or no changes in relation to the domains of health and well-being, relationships, quality of life, choice and control, participation in community life, feeling of security at home, personal dignity in support, and economic well-being (Carr and Robbins, 2009). However, the authors of this evaluation stressed that the study had limitations as the sample was not necessarily representative, and people with learning disabilities or physical disabilities were more likely to report improvements than the small numbers of older people who participated (Glasby and Littlechild, 2009).

More recently, In Control has published an evaluation of the third phase, from 2008 to 2009. Over two-thirds of the local authorities participating in this evaluation provided a breakdown of personal budget recipients by service user group, indicating that 23 per cent had physical disabilities, 18 per cent had learning disabilities, 6 per cent had mental health problems, and older people represented the remaining 53 per cent. The aggregated findings from this phase and phase two are presented (Tyson et al., 2010). The resulting data are not subdivided into service user groups. Rather, the results are presented as data relating to the overall uptake of personal budgets from a participant group of between 385 and 522 people, and the impact of these personal budgets on their lives. The findings are positive, with 66 per cent of the participant group reporting that the control they had over their support had improved, and 68 per cent reporting that their overall quality of life had improved since receiving personal budgets; 58 per cent reported spending more time with people they wanted to, and also taking a more active role in their community; 55 per cent felt they were supported with more dignity, and 51 per cent reported feeling in better health.

Service user groups

People with learning disabilities

The Ibsen study identified mixed results for this service user group. Service users and their carers reported that the individual budget process itself was stressful – possibly accentuated by the length of time required during the pilot to put an individual budget into place. However, service users reported higher levels of psychological well-being, possibly linked to using their budgets for leisure and social participation activities, with subsequent benefits to well-being. Of all the service user groups in this study, people with learning disabilities were more likely to report having control over their daily lives as a result of the individual budget (Glendinning et al., 2008).

A possible explanation given for these mixed results, or to explain why outcomes were not more positive for this group, is that many of these service users may have experienced person-centred planning (PCP) previously, and therefore would not have experienced self-directed planning as such a radical shift in approach. It is important to keep in mind that personal budgets were essentially born of a desire to improve services for people with learning disabilities, building on the principles of person-centred planning and self-advocacy, and the aims enshrined in *Valuing people* (DH, 2001), in which the government had articulated its plans for learning disability services. Hence there was already a firm foundation of a person-centred and inclusive approach to the provision of services for this particular service user group which was not so prevalent in other service user groups.

The evaluations conducted by In Control had overall more positive findings for this service user group. Their evaluation of the second phase, from 2005 to 2007, was based on interviews with 196 participants using self-directed support (Hatton et al., 2008). Of this participant group, 58 per cent had learning disabilities, and while the resulting data were not subdivided into specific service user groups, the overall findings give a reliable indication of the level of satisfaction experienced by the 58 per cent of the group who had learning disabilities. Table 4.1 summarises the outcomes for all participants.

Table 4.1 *Outcomes*

	Improvement (%)	Same (%)	Worse (%)
General health and well-being	47	48	5
Spending time with people you like	55	42	3
Quality of life	76	23	1
Taking part in and contributing to the community	64	34	2
Choice and control	72	27	1
Feeling safe and secure at home	29	70	1
Personal dignity	59	41	0
Economic well-being	36	59	5

(Source: Hatton et al., 2008)

People with learning disabilities were more likely to report improvements in their quality of life if this was their first experience of receiving support – that is, in instances where they had not been receiving social care support prior to using personal budgets. This substantiates the hypothesis that the mixed results in the Ibsen study were a reflection of positive previous experiences of person-centred planning, rather than negative experiences of individual budgets or self-directed support.

Along with people with physical disabilities, people with learning disabilities were found to be more likely than other service user groups to report improvements in their abilities to participate in and/or contribute to their local communities. Similarly, these two service user groups were more likely to report improvements in choice and control in relation to their support, along with improvements in their economic well-being. In relation to personal dignity, older people with learning disabilities were more likely to report improvements than younger people with learning disabilities.

It is encouraging that even though this service user group identified the process of individual budgets as inherently stressful, it appears that once the individual budget was actually in place, their abilities to direct their own support were clearly evident. This refutes initial concerns raised when direct payments were first being introduced in 1996, that people with learning disabilities would be unable to manage their payments – concerns that unfortunately contributed to minimal uptake of direct payments by this service user group, particularly prior to the publication of *Valuing people* in 2001 (Gardner, 1999; DH, 2001).

ACTIVITY 4.1

David is a 19-year-old man who has a learning disability. He lives with his parents, and he has recently been informed that he is eligible to apply for a personal budget. He has heard about these from his friends at the day centre he attends, and he wants to use part of his budget to travel on public transport so that he can attend activities in the city centre. David's parents feel overwhelmed by this development. They are happy with his current care package, which involves David attending a local authority day centre five days a week. They have no knowledge of any other services, and don't know where to start.

• *If you were the social worker involved here, how would you approach this?*

• *Are there any particular social work skills that you might use?*

COMMENT

You may have considered using active listening skills, to ensure that you communicated your understanding of David's wishes, alongside his parents' concerns. You may have considered providing accurate and clearly accessible information about the personal budget process, explaining how you could help David and his parents navigate their way through this process.

In considering this activity, you will have recognised that there is a vital role for professionals at this stage of the process, to ensure that any concerns are addressed as early as possible, rather than allowing these to become major disincentives for service users and their carers.

The local authority circular *Transforming social care* (DH, 2008a) acknowledges that a personalised approach to social care will require radical changes within the social care workforce. Social workers in the adult social care field, who had previously become disillusioned with their care management roles, have welcomed the possibility of providing more personalised support services, and practising in ways that are in accordance with their professional value base (Tyson et al., 2010). As part of its Total Transformation project, In Control carried out some work to determine whether social workers have a distinctive role within a system of self-directed support, recognising that the ethos and values of the social work profession align closely with the philosophy of self-directed support (Tyson, 2009) The findings indicate that while the various tasks involved cannot only or always be carried out by social workers, in practice social workers are often best placed to carry out these tasks. For example, in relation to assisting service users to devise a support plan, the findings highlight that social workers are trained *to help people to assess, manage and take appropriate risks … and to assist with more person-centred ways of managing risk* (Tyson, 2009, p. 7). With this in mind, consider the following activity.

Continuing with the case scenario from the last activity, you are now presented with further information. Thanks to your input so far, David and his parents now understand how the personal budget can be used. However, David's parents are opposed to David using his budget to access public transport and attend activities in the city centre. They consider that their son has no road sense, and that he would be frightened by the crowds and noise in the city.

• *Can you identify any issues in this scenario that may call on social work skills to assist with more person centred ways of managing risk (Tyson, 2009, p. 7)?*

• *Are there any elements of your social work value base and codes of practice that provide guidance for you?*

COMMENT

You may have recognised that David's parents possibly need help in coming to terms with David's transition into adulthood, which will include him making decisions for himself, albeit with support to enable him to make informed decisions.

You may have identified that you would need to spend time with David and his parents in order to facilitate a discussion about potential risks, and to consider risk management strategies.

You may have acknowledged that the code of practice requires you to promote the independence of service users while protecting them as far as possible from danger or harm. *We will look at ways to work in accordance with the codes of practice within the context of personalisation in more detail in Chapter 7.*

People with physical and sensory disabilities

People with physical and sensory disabilities belong to a service user group that has a long history of collective action in order to challenge the discrimination experienced by disabled people in British society. This service user group began to organise itself politically during the nineteenth century, with the British Deaf Association being founded in 1890. As you saw in Chapter 2, several key organisations controlled by disabled people rather than for them were established from the 1970s onwards, seeking social change and social justice. These organisations, from the Union of the Physically Impaired against Segregation (UPIAS), established in 1971, through to the British Council of Organisations of Disabled People (BCODP), established in 1981, were championed by disabled people, who led the campaign for independent living, established Centres for Independent Living, and promoted the case for direct payments (Glasby et al., 2006).

The Ibsen study identified that people with physical or sensory disabilities of working age had overall more positive experiences of individual budgets, with positive effects on all dimensions of social care outcomes, but particularly reporting receiving better quality care, and greater satisfaction with the support received. There are a number of factors that may have influenced these findings. This service user group already included the majority of recipients of direct payments (Glasby et al., 2006), and therefore collectively had a range of experience relating to the process of self-directed support. Also, the levels of individual budgets allocated to this service user group were comparatively higher than those for other service user groups, consequently allowing for greater flexibility, and essentially more resources with which to purchase higher quality and/or more specialised support services (Glendinning et al., 2008).

As I outlined earlier, the evaluation carried out by In Control of their second phase, 2005–2007, identified a number of positive findings which related specifically to people with learning disabilities and people with physical disabilities. It is not necessary to repeat the findings here, but suffice to say that they reaffirm the above results from the Ibsen study (Hatton et al., 2008).

ACTIVITY **4.3**

At this point, you may find it useful to plot out a timeline of developments in relation to the political activities of this service user group. If possible, try to find out if any organisations run by and for disabled people have been established in your local area and, if so, what information and other services do they provide for potential individual budget users? A good starting point for your enquiries is the National Centre for Independent Living website, available at www.ncil.org.uk/

Older people

There are currently 12 million people aged over 65 in the UK, and this number is expected to rise to 15.8 million by 2031 (DH, 2010b). Older people currently constitute the largest service user group receiving social care support, and they are now the largest group in receipt of personal budgets (DH, 2010b, 2008d).

There have been more concerns raised by more people in relation to individual budgets for older people than for any other service user group. The results from the Ibsen study for this service user group were less positive than for the other service user groups, and reinforced concerns about the benefits of individual budgets for older people. Crucially, older people with individual budgets reported lower levels of psychological well-being than their comparison group. The researchers proposed that this may have been due to their anxiety about changes to current support arrangements, and concerns about assuming administrative responsibilities for their support, added to the fact that older people often contacted services when in crisis, and consequently at times when they were least able to derive maximum benefit from self-directed support (Glendinning et al., 2008).

Older people tended to use their individual budgets for high levels of assistance with personal care, rather than for leisure and social participation activities, whereas it has been demonstrated in relation to people with learning disabilities that participation in social activities tends to lead to improvements in psychological well-being. Older people also received smaller levels of individual budgets, compared with younger adults with physical or learning disabilities, and this will have significantly restricted their abilities to use the individual budgets flexibly (Glendinning et al., 2008).

All of these factors may have contributed to a significant proportion of the older people concerned (39 per cent) who had already been in receipt of a social care package reporting that they had not and were not planning to make any changes to their previous social care package despite now receiving an individual budget. In this type of scenario, it is easy to see where an individual budget and the associated administrative responsibilities represent a burden rather than a liberation (Hasler, 2006).

Given that it was estimated that by the end of March 2010 there would be approximately 206,000 people in receipt of personal budgets, and that 40 per cent of all service users would be older people, it is understandable that the Department of Health's initial response to the Ibsen findings considers in some detail the issues raised in relation to older people (DH, 2008e). This publication highlights the importance of good support to help older people access and benefit from individual budgets.

The findings from the Ibsen study need to be considered alongside the evaluation results from In Control's second phase (Hatton et al., 2008). These results identified that older people were more likely to report improvement in their quality of life, the choice and control they had over their lives, and their personal dignity, if they had been supported by a social worker in planning their self-directed support.

This evaluation also found that compared with other service user groups, older people were less likely to have been in receipt of social care prior to receiving a personal budget. This links to the factor highlighted in the Ibsen study, that older people frequently approach services when they are in crisis. Therefore it is almost self-explanatory that for any service user approaching services for the first time, in a state of crisis with all the associated feelings of vulnerability and possibly confusion about what services are available, then professional support with planning is crucial to the success of self-directed support. Expecting service users to do everything for themselves is not how the pioneers of direct payments and independent living envisaged developments (Hasler, 2006).

The theme of adequate support with planning appears in several key documents relating to personalisation, highlighting that with proper support, personal budgets can work well for older people (DH, 2008a, 2008d, 2010b). This message is reinforced in the recent publication providing guidance for brokers and support planners (DH, 2010c). However, the thorny issue regarding who is best placed to provide this brokerage and support is only partially addressed: *There are a variety of ways and a range of different people who can provide assistance in support planning and brokerage* (DH, 2010c, p. 3). This somewhat contradicts an earlier statement regarding the social work role within personalised services, which indicated that *the role of social workers will be focused on advocacy and brokerage, rather than assessment and gate keeping* (DH, 2008a, p. 4).

So, while the In Control findings seem to point towards social workers as the professionals best suited to carry out these support planning and brokerage functions, particularly in relation to older people, there continues to be a lot of uncertainty about a definitive role for social workers. As you saw in Chapter 3, the debate regarding the location of brokerage services, and whether these need to be located outside the statutory sector, continues. While there is a recognition of the value of independent support, this is offset by concerns relating to lack of regulation and professionalism (Scourfield, 2010).

ACTIVITY 4.4

The findings from these evaluations indicate that older people potentially require additional support, to enable this service user group to maximise the opportunities inherent in self-directed support.

- *Can you envisage a role for social workers within the support planning and brokerage arena for older people?*

- *Can you identify any social work skills that would be particularly useful when working with this service user group?*

COMMENT

You may have identified the knowledge that social workers have regarding community resources and local services, and also their networking skills and abilities to engage with a wide range of service providers.

You may have considered the social work skills and experience in direct work associated with care management tasks – organising and implementing care plans, negotiating with service providers, and reviewing outcomes. These skills are transferable to the person-centred planning that is the cornerstone of self-directed support, with the proviso that social workers fully embrace and apply the principles of choice, control and empowerment that underpin the personalisation agenda.

People with mental health problems

People with mental health problems have historically been the least well served by initiatives aimed at increasing choice and control, for example direct payments. Following a report from the Social Exclusion Unit (2004), guidance was commissioned by the government to address the worryingly low take-up of direct payments by people with mental health problems (NIMHE, 2006). This guidance revealed that in March 2005, almost a quarter of local authorities in England were not making direct payments to this service user group at all, and another half of the remaining local authorities were only making between one and five direct payments (NIMHE, 2006). It was clear that this needed to be addressed, and the aim of the guidance was to *promote direct payments within mental health services as a means of facilitating greater social participation* (NIMHE, 2006, p. 4). Other work has also been conducted by the Health and Social Care Advisory Service (HASCAS) to promote the use of direct payments by people with mental health problems (Newbigging with Lowe, 2005).

Encouragingly, the Ibsen study found that mental health service users in receipt of individual budgets reported the most positive outcomes in overall well-being, and significantly higher quality of life. This service user group benefited from the flexibility of individual budgets which enabled them to access a greater range of support services, as opposed to standard services (Glendinning et al., 2008).

However, it was notable that mental health service users represented only 14 per cent of individual budget users in this study, and this was addressed in the Department of

Health's initial response to the Ibsen study (DH, 2008e). This response identified several key barriers to the effective take-up of individual budgets for this group of service users, and instigated a range of activities to address these barriers. These included the production and dissemination of information about individual budgets, examples of best practice, and examples of how advanced councils and primary care trusts have worked through organisational barriers (DH, 2008e). One such publication is the *Paths to personalisation*, a whole-system guide to clarify what changes are required, *to make personalisation a reality for people with mental health needs* (National Mental Health Development Unit, 2010, p. 6). This comprehensive guide addresses all areas of self-directed support, and is aligned with the recommendations of *New horizons* (DH, 2009b), the cross-government mental health strategy, which aims to improve the mental health of the population and also to improve mental health services (NMHDU, 2010).

The Ibsen study identified professional attitudes as one of the main barriers to the take-up of individual budgets for this service user group (DH, 2008e), echoing findings from previous research into the low take-up of direct payments by people with mental health problems (Ridley and Jones, 2003). It has been emphasised elsewhere that the cultural shift which is now required within the professional mental health field must not be underestimated, with the current mental health system being *characterized by both authoritarian risk-aversion and disabling paternalism* (Coppock and Dunn, 2010, p. 58). The *Paths to personalisation* guide (NMHDU, 2010) addresses the issue of risk and risk management by proposing that positive risk taking can be achieved by supporting service users to make provisions in advance of their mental health fluctuating, by making advance directives and crisis management plans. The advantages of this type of risk management, whereby risk management strategies are devised and therefore owned by the individual service user, have been recognised and welcomed by participants in the Mind project Putting Us First (Heslop and Williams, 2010a). This project, which ran from October 2008 to March 2010, aimed to reduce barriers to personalisation, particularly professional attitudes, and therefore increase the take-up of personal budgets among mental health service users.

For mental health professionals, supporting service users to maintain choice and control when their mental health may fluctuate represents a major challenge (SCIE, 2009). Mental health professionals will be required to support positive risk taking alongside requirements to safeguard vulnerable adults, all the time aware of the public perception that no level of risk is acceptable for people with mental health needs, in sharp contrast to the risks that non-service users can take freely.

The Care Programme Approach was introduced in 1990 as the collaborative mechanism between health and local authorities to provide for the health and social care needs of people with mental health problems (Braye and Preston-Shoot, 2010). Within this legislative framework, the role of the care co-ordinator is seen as pivotal, and this role is most frequently carried out by either social workers or community psychiatric nurses (DH, 2008f). Putting Us First (Heslop and Williams, 2010b) provides a guide for care co-ordinators, who are seen as central to the cultural shift that is required in order to make personalisation a reality for people with mental health needs.

ACTIVITY *4.5*

You are a social worker on a multi-disciplinary community mental health team, and you are the care co-ordinator for Yasmin, a service user who has fluctuating mental health needs. When she is well, she lives independently, with minimal support requirements, but when she is unwell, she becomes unable to eat, drink or care for herself without intensive support. In the past, this has always resulted in hospital admission. Yasmin is currently well, and she wants to avoid another hospital admission.

* *How might you approach working with Yasmin within the context of a self-directed, personalised approach? For this exercise you will find it useful to consult the Mind guide for care co-ordinators (Heslop and Williams, 2010b).*

COMMENT

Within the Mind guide for care co-ordinators, you will have seen that drawing up a risk or crisis management plan forms an integral part of the process of self-directed support. You may have thought about helping Yasmin to work out a crisis contingency plan for her support workers, which could include signs that would indicate to her support workers that she may be becoming unwell, and an advance statement detailing what actions they should take if this happens. For example, she may want her support workers to contact you as her care co-ordinator, so that you can organise additional support for her at home at these times. As part of the support planning process, you will have explained to Yasmin how she can 'bank' her support for times when it is needed most. This is one of the advantages of the flexible ways in which personal budgets can be used, which really accommodates service users who have fluctuating support needs.

Personalisation is closely aligned with the social model of disability and with the recovery approach to mental health problems and consequently sits comfortably alongside the social work value base and codes of practice (GSCC, 2002). Since social workers have a history of working in partnership with service users and are committed to anti-oppressive and anti-discriminatory practice, they have a valid contribution to make, in order to bring about the cultural change that is required in the mental health field. This is encouraging, because within the mental health field social workers have traditionally held a rather ambiguous position, caught between the dominant professional discipline of psychiatry and mainstream social work (Walton, 1999).

The social work role has become increasingly marginalised in contemporary mental health law and policy, with the emphasis now on integrated inter-professional teams, and more controversially with the Mental Health Act 2007 replacing the role of the Approved Social Worker with that of the Approved Mental Health Professional (DH, 2007c). Therefore it could be argued that it is imperative for mental health social workers to actively progress the implementation of the personalisation agenda, both for the benefit of service users and also to secure their professional position within a changing workforce.

ACTIVITY **4.6**

There have been some very positive responses from the service users who took part in the *Putting Us First* project, indicating that the quality of support received from care co-ordinators was very important in order to achieve their desired outcomes, and that care co-ordinators have an important role in enabling mental health service users to access mainstream community activities (Heslop and Williams, 2010b).

In Chapter 2, the issue was raised that one of the recommendations of the Social Work Task Force, to elevate social work to a new level of professionalism (DH, 2009a), could be viewed as a contradiction to the personalisation agenda (Leece and Leece, 2010).

• Using the above findings as a starting point, can you identify ways to approach this apparent contradiction?

COMMENT

You may have highlighted the benefits of social work knowledge and skills similar to those identified in Activity 4.4, relating to social work knowledge of community resources, and skills in liaising with a wide range of providers. You will probably have recognised that there is also considerable skill involved in ensuring that the service user retains control over the whole process, while you retain your role as an advocate, as and when required.

Parents of disabled children

The introduction of the Carers and Disabled Children Act in 2000 extended direct payments to include parents of disabled children. Although there has been a relatively slow take-up of direct payments since then by this group, a study carried out by Blyth and Gardner found that families who used direct payments were able to take control of the support received, indicating that direct payments apply equally to children as well as adults (Blyth and Gardner, 2007). It has been argued elsewhere that personalisation and self-directed support should start as soon as a child or young person is identified as needing additional support, and should form part of a 'whole-life' approach (Crosby, 2008).

The government made a commitment to pilot individual budgets for families with disabled children, outlined in *Aiming high for disabled children: Better support for families* (HM Treasury and DCSF, 2007). Prior to this pilot commencing, a scoping study was conducted to review the approaches that were already being used to deliver individual budgets or other self-directed support initiatives for this service user group (Prabhakar *et al.*, 2008). The approaches that were identified in this study included the following.

• *Dynamite* Self-directed futures for young people. This two-year programme worked with 12 local authorities to develop self-directed support for young disabled people aged 14–25 years, as they made the transition to adulthood. This programme was led by Paradigm, an In Control partner agency.

- *Taking Control* This ongoing project represents In Control's programme of self-directed support for disabled children and young people aged 0–18 years.

- *Budget Holding Lead Professionals* This pilot took place from June 2006 to March 2008, in which identified lead professionals were given the opportunity to manage small budgets on behalf of families with children who had additional needs.

- *Ibsen study* A number of families with disabled young people aged 16–18 years formed part of the service users who took part in this national evaluation.

(Prabhakar et al., 2008; Crosby, 2006)

A number of issues relating to these early initiatives were identified in the scoping study that would need to be addressed in the proposed individual budget pilot. These included that pilot sites that had limited choice of management of individual budget funds or support brokerage predominantly attracted families from middle-class backgrounds. Also, some staff involved in the Taking Control and Dynamite projects had raised concern about their capacity to take on additional work. The scoping study also involved a consultation exercise, which found that families were deterred from taking up direct payments because they did not want the responsibility of managing their own budget, or of becoming an employer (Prabhakar et al., 2008).

REFLECTION POINT

For busy social workers, even contemplating taking on additional tasks can seem daunting, and this can result in an unconscious reinforcing of families' concerns about taking on extra responsibilities. It is vital, therefore, that as a social worker you continually explore and question your ways of working with service users and carers, to ensure that you are working in their best interests. In relation to self-directed support, as this may result in additional work in the short term, it is important for social workers to discuss workload issues with their line managers, and perhaps to negotiate additional time for supporting service users who want to engage with self-directed support.

The actual pilot for individual budgets for families with disabled children commenced in April 2009 and is due to run until March 2011, with a possible period of extension to March 2012, subject to funding (Prabhakar et al., 2010). The pilot involves six local authorities and primary care trusts setting up and delivering individual budgets for families with disabled children, and aims to establish whether individual budgets:

- enable this group to have greater choice and control over their support package;

- improve outcomes for some or all of this group, compared with traditional service provision;

- lead to increased levels of satisfaction for some or all of this group.

The pilot also aims to identify any unintended consequences or barriers experienced by local authorities or primary care trusts in the implementation of individual budgets for this group (Prabhakar et al., 2010).

The families involved in this pilot consist of a diverse group in relation to the nature of the child/young person's disability, the socio-economic status of the family, and any previous experience of personalised approaches. The authors conclude from this that personalised approaches may well appeal across the social spectrum, therefore delivering high-quality support to a diverse range of families with disabled children (Prabhakar et al., 2010).

CASE STUDY

Mrs Jones has a 12-year-old daughter, Sarah, who has autism and severe learning difficulties. Sarah used to attend a day centre for two days each week, but the noise and the number of people at the centre upset her, and she would be distressed for several days after attending the centre.

The family's social worker spent time with Mrs Jones and Sarah, explaining about individual budgets, and how self-directed support could operate in practice for Sarah. The individual budget was subsequently put in place, and following negotiation with her line manager, the social worker was able to allocate additional time to assist this family with support planning and brokerage. Six months later, Mrs Jones has begun to employ several personal assistants who spend time with Sarah each day, accompanying her to educational and leisure facilities in the local community. Mrs Jones reports that Sarah is much more relaxed now, and that this has had a beneficial effect on the rest of the family also.

COMMENT

This case illustrates the benefits for service users and carers, when social workers are able to practise within a personalisation context, which may involve some negotiation with line managers regarding workload.

The early findings after the first year of this pilot indicate that there have been mixed reactions from families regarding their indicative budgets, particularly where the indicative budget proved to be less than the traditional service budget. While some families found that their individual budget resource could purchase more than they had anticipated, due to the lower employment costs of personal assistants, other families required assistance with detailed support planning, in order to achieve their outcomes with smaller budgetary resources. A small proportion of families (eight in total) dropped out of the pilot because of their lower indicative budget allocation (Prabhakar et al., 2010). Similar findings are evident in the Ibsen study, where families were concerned that lower individual budgets would place additional burdens on family members to supplement provision with more unpaid informal care (Rabiee et al., 2009).

On a more positive note, families taking part in the current pilot reported feeling listened to, and being properly engaged in support planning for the first time (Prabhakar et al., 2010). The full evaluation of this pilot in 2011 will contain feedback from families who will by then have been using their individual budgets for approximately eight months, and will contain more comprehensive data on levels of service user satisfaction, any improvements in outcomes and any improvements in choice and control in relation to support packages.

Service users with multiple and complex needs

While there is no absolute consensus regarding which service users are included under this heading, the term usually refers to people who present with a range of different needs requiring support from several service providers, and some of these needs may be severe or profound (CSCI, 2009). The numbers of people with multiple and complex needs are relatively small, but the costs of meeting these needs can be high. The resulting service provision can prove to be standardised rather than individualised, often involving remote out-of-area service provision, for example specialist residential placements. In addition to being inappropriate, out-of-area provision is expensive, and diverts funds which could be used to develop local service provision (Henwood and Hudson, 2009; CSCI, 2009). The personalisation agenda aims to transform service provision for all service users, yet it appears that people with complex needs remain on the periphery of this emerging agenda.

Concerns have been expressed that personalisation and self-directed support are more accessible for articulate service users who can specify their needs and preferences, which could lead to inequity (Henwood and Hudson, 2009). Conversely, in a review by the think tank Demos, the argument is put forward that personal budgets actually create more equity than the current system, which already *rewards the most articulate at the expense of the less confident* (Leadbeater et al., 2008, p. 47). Personalised support plans, based on a transparent system of resource allocation, have the potential to include more service user groups, including those who possibly require additional support with self-assessment and support planning (Leadbeater et al., 2008).

In the study commissioned by CSCI to explore five councils' responses to people with complex needs, Henwood and Hudson found that while some councils were endeavouring to deliver personalisation for people with complex needs, most councils involved in the study were focused on service users with less complex needs and more easily achievable outcomes (Henwood and Hudson, 2009). The findings indicate a general misgiving that self-directed support approaches have not been adequately developed for people with complex needs, possibly linked to the intensive support required from professionals with the self-assessment process, which was considered more time-consuming than traditional professional assessment.

ACTIVITY 4.7

At this stage it would be useful for you to read the CSCI report (Henwood and Hudson, 2009), available at www.csci.org.uk, as it provides a detailed articulation of the specific issues related to personalisation for people with complex needs. It also contains some very informative case studies that illustrate some experiences of service users with complex needs, and those of their carers.

Another area that was highlighted in this study related to funding these higher-cost support packages. Difficulties already identified in the Ibsen study regarding the integration of different funding streams are perhaps even more pertinent for people with complex support needs that cross organisational boundaries (Glendinning et al., 2008; CSCI, 2009). Some of these difficulties may be addressed in the current personal health budget pilot programme (DH, 2009c). Personal health budgets are being piloted at present in 70 sites in England, with 20 of these sites participating in an in-depth evaluation. The pilot commenced in April 2009, and will run until April 2012. Initial findings based on interviews with project leads indicate that there are a number of challenges including budget-setting, care planning, cultural change, integration of health and social care, and the impact on the workplace (Jones et al., 2010a). There are no reports as yet related to the experiences of service users in receipt of personal health budgets.

Therefore, there may be additional challenges inherent in ensuring that the personalisation agenda includes people with multiple and complex needs.

Under-represented groups

It is also apparent that there are challenges to be faced in order to ensure that personalisation and self-directed support become a reality for other service user groups who are currently under-represented within social care services. The experiences of service users and carers from black and minority ethnic communities indicate that these service users face additional barriers, and hence are disproportionately poorly represented in statistics related to the take-up of direct payments. Research carried out by SCIE highlights that there are no official data specifically relating to the take-up of direct payments by black and minority ethnic service users – representative of the general inadequate level of attention paid to this section of the UK population (Carr and Robbins, 2009; Stuart, 2006). The Direct Payments Development Fund, established in 2003 to make funding available to develop projects specifically aimed at addressing low take-up of direct payments, identified a similar scarcity of information relating to the barriers experienced by black and minority ethnic groups in relation to direct payments (Wilson and Gilbert, 2006).

The examination by Stuart (2006) of the experiences of black and minority ethnic service users in relation to the take-up of direct payments identified that assessment processes do not adequately take account of these service users' backgrounds and particular requirements; that linguistic barriers represent the biggest obstacles; that difficulties exist in trying to recruit suitable personal assistants who can meet the cultural, linguistic and religious needs of these service users; and that service users are not informed about how to access direct payments; alongside insufficient support and advocacy services (Stuart, 2006). In the Ibsen study, black and minority ethnic groups represented 8 per cent of the total sample group, but the resulting data were not broken down in a way to reflect the experiences of these groups in relation to receiving individual budgets (Glendinning et al., 2008).

ACTIVITY **4.8**

In one of its reports which aim to help employers meet the personalisation agenda by addressing equality and diversity issues (CSCI, 2008a), the CSCI has highlighted the issue that black and minority ethnic service users do not have adequate information about direct payments or personal budgets, and need more support and advocacy, if they are to be empowered to arrange their care in this way.

*   *During your practice placements, try to establish how information about direct payments and personal budgets is disseminated in the local community.*

Continued

ACTIVITY *4.8* *continued*

- *Can you think of ways to publicise information to ensure that is easily accessible by black and minority ethnic groups?*

- *You will need to consider not just how information is made available, but also where it is made available.*

COMMENT

You will probably have thought about providing information in languages that reflect the diversity of the local community, and also in formats other than the written word. You may have identified that it is important not to assume that people from black and minority ethnic groups will regularly visit community spaces (for example libraries), and that it is vital that information about personal budgets and other social care services is made available in culturally appropriate community spaces.

From the outset, the work of In Control has been based on a belief that personalisation is an approach for all service users, but that in order to realistically achieve this aspiration, flexible models would need to be developed to meet the needs of the diverse cultures and groups within society. In the report on their third phase, In Control have included some examples of innovative projects that illustrate how local authorities and service providers are implementing self-directed support in ways that include under-represented groups, which I would encourage the reader to refer to (Tyson et al., 2010).

There are no data which specifically examine the impact of direct payments or personal budgets for lesbian and gay people, who may present with additional needs in relation to self-directed support (Carr and Robbins, 2009). Encouragingly though, in another of the reports from the CSCI relating to the implementation of the personalisation agenda, a survey carried out indicates that direct payments or personal budgets could improve choice and control for these service users. Levels of satisfaction were found to be higher for lesbian and gay people using direct payments, compared with those in receipt of traditional service provision (CSCI, 2008b). These higher levels of satisfaction were linked to lesbian and gay people having choice over the workers employed; being able to arrange support flexibly; and having the control to decide what action to take if a worker behaved in a discriminatory manner.

Other service users who may require further assistance to ensure that they are included in the personalisation agenda include those living in rural areas, as opinion continues to be divided regarding the implications for people in these areas (Glasby and Littlechild, 2009). An Audit Commission survey of local authorities conducted in 2006 found some evidence that direct payments could supplement total provision in rural areas, where contract agencies found it uneconomical to operate (Audit Commission, 2006, cited in Carr and Robbins, 2009, p. 17). However, a research briefing produced by the SCIE raised concerns that the move to self-directed support in rural areas could lead to recruitment problems (Pugh et al., 2007), but perhaps, as Leadbeater and co-authors argue, this is not insurmountable. They base this assertion on the high take-up of direct payments in the Orkney Islands in Scotland, where people have used direct payments to good effect, in order to formulate localised solutions (Leadbeater et al., 2008). As the authors argue in this Demos report, the potential exists for self-directed services to work for service users from all under-represented groups, because people are empowered to create solutions that work for them.

Impact on carers

The original Ibsen study focused on the impact of individual budgets on service users and didn't explore the potential impact on carers. Therefore a follow-up study was conducted in 2009, which examined the impact on carers of service users in receipt of individual budgets (Glendinning et al., 2009). The full report is available at www.york.ac.uk/spru, and as with the original Ibsen study, it is important that you consult the full report, as I am only providing a summary here.

This study identified that carers of service users in receipt of individual budgets were far more likely to have been involved in the support planning, compared with carers of people in receipt of conventional services. Carers of people with learning difficulties were particularly likely to report a greater level of involvement in the support planning process, while carers of older people were more likely to report that their own needs were also taken into account as part of the support planning process. There were positive impacts on carers' quality of life and social care outcomes, partly due to carers being able to engage in activities of their choice, because someone could be paid to carry out some of the tasks they had previously done. There was also a beneficial effect on the carers' quality of life if the individual budget resulted in better quality of life for the service user (Glendinning et al., 2009).

These very positive findings need to be considered alongside some more problematic issues. The study revealed that the monetary value of individual budgets was lower if help from informal carers was taken into account, which could be seen as penalising informal carers. This study also revealed some worrying findings in relation to payments made directly to carers from the individual budgets awarded. This only occurred in a small number of cases, but even in this minority very mixed feelings were expressed. Generally carers considered it inappropriate to pay family members for the care provided, and there were variations between the pilot sites, with some permitting payments to co-resident carers, while others considered this contravened the direct payments guidelines which informed the individual budget pilot. However, it could be argued that the revised guidelines, while not exactly encouraging payments to co-resident carers, at least now sanction these where necessary to meet the service users' needs (DH, 2003a).

Of the carers in this study who received a payment from service users' individual budgets payments, these were either minimal (approximately £5.00 per month) or paid for only a small proportion of the care provided. The carers concerned all reported that the payment was not the incentive to provide the care, and while a couple of carers considered the payment helpful, others felt it was inadequate (Glendinning et al., 2009).

ACTIVITY *4.9*

- *Can you identify strategies which you, as a professional social worker, could employ to try to ensure that informal carers are not overused or unacknowledged?*

- *Is there any element of the code of practice that is relevant here? Do the strategies you have identified enable you to practise in accordance with this element?*

COMMENT

Strategies could include ensuring that carers are actively involved in all aspects of the personal budget process, that their own needs are recognised and then addressed, and that they are made aware of all payments they may be entitled to. You may have explored the gender inequalities that exist in relation to informal caring – given that the majority of informal carers are women, and that their caring responsibilities can have an adverse affect on their employment prospects and subsequent income. You will have highlighted that the code of practice requires you to protect the rights and promote the interests of service users and carers *(GSCC, 2002). However, as you saw in Activity 4.2, service users and their carers can have different and sometimes opposing interests, and consequently your work may at times involve trying to find ways to reconcile these differences, or to negotiate a compromise.*

This initial follow-up study has certainly highlighted the need for further research regarding the impact of individual budgets on carers, particularly in relation to payments made to carers from individual budgets and how these payments would align with other statutory carer entitlements (Glendinning et al., 2009). One of the criticisms concerning personalisation is that it could be used to reduce public spending (Adams, 2010). Ensuring that informal carers are paid, whatever the mechanism used, could be one way of ensuring that the more altruistic motivations for personalisation dominate.

CHAPTER SUMMARY

In this chapter you have reviewed the experience of personalisation from the perspectives of the different service user groups, drawing on statistical information from several evaluations that have been carried out. You will now be familiar with the different experiences that services users have reported, and with some of the hypotheses put forward to explain the different outcomes among these different service user groups.

In this chapter you have also been encouraged to consider the social work role within the context of personalised services, a subject that will be considered in more detail in Chapter 7. It is clear that there are challenges ahead for social work within personalised services, but there are indications from service users that support from social workers can be highly beneficial in relation to self-directed support.

Glasby, J and Littlechild, R (2009) *Direct payments and personal budgets. Putting personalisation into practice.* Bristol: Policy Press.

This book is an invaluable resource for everyone interested in personalisation. It summarises the current evidence in relation to direct payments and personal budgets, and considers some of the challenges inherent in the implementation of self-directed support.

Leece, J and Bornat, J (eds) (2006) *Developments in direct payments.* Bristol: Policy Press.

This book provides you with the opportunity to consider and compare the experiences of providers and service users in relation to direct payments. It also compares developments in the UK with those in North America.

National Mental Health Development Unit (NMHDU) (2010) *Paths to personalisation.* London: DH.

This guide has been produced to help explain what changes are needed, in order to make personalisation a reality for people with mental health needs. It provides examples of good practice, and signposts the reader to some excellent sources of advice and information.

WEBSITES

www.in-control.org.uk

This website contains a wealth of information relating to policy, practice and experience from people directing their own support.

www.york.ac.uk/spru

The Social Policy Research Unit has an international reputation for excellence in research. This website contains many of the key studies and also useful articles relating to personalisation.

www.ncil.org.uk

The National Centre for Independent Living website contains valuable information relating to independent living, direct payments and personal budgets.

Chapter 5
Service user narrative

This chapter will begin to help you meet the following National Occupational Standards.

Key role 1: Prepare for, and work with individuals, families, carers, groups and communities to assess their needs and circumstances.

- Work with individuals, families, carers, groups and communities to identify, gather, analyse and understand information.
- Work with individuals, families, carers, groups and communities to enable them to analyse, identify, clarify and express their strengths, expectations and limitations.
- Work with individuals, families and carers, groups and communities to enable them to assess and make informed decisions about their needs, circumstances, risks, preferred options and resources.

Also important here are the General Social Care Council Codes of Practice for social care employers (GSCC, 2002), which state the following.

Social care workers must protect the rights and promote the interests of service users and carers; this includes:

- Treating each person as an individual (1.1).
- Respecting and, where appropriate, promoting the individual views and wishes of both service users and carers (1.2).
- Supporting service users' rights to control their lives and make informed choices about the services they receive (1.3).
- Respecting diversity and different cultures and values (1.6).

As a social care worker, you must promote the independence of service users while protecting them as far as possible from danger or harm.

- Promoting the independence of service users and assisting them to understand and exercise their rights (3.1).
- Recognising and using responsibly the power that comes from your work with service users and carers (3.8).

The chapter will also introduce you to the following academic standards set out in the 2008 social work subject benchmark statement.

5.5.3 Analysis and synthesis.
5.6 Communication skills.

Introduction

This chapter provides an opportunity to hear directly from individuals directing their own support. It would be impossible to write a book about personalisation without contributions from individuals. Listening to their experiences provides us with an opportunity to gain some insight into how this agenda is changing the lives of individuals in need of social care.

Social work textbooks regularly provide case studies to aid student learning. Typically students are given a set of circumstances followed by a number of questions in relation to the social work role. In seminars, it is common for students to be asked to break into small groups and work through information, suggesting how the social worker should intervene to support the individual in need. We must, however, acknowledge that the relationship being crafted here between social worker and service user is based on an underlying assumption that the social worker knows best. In this process of learning, students are being trained to respond to information rather than individuals. This probably seems a little strange as many of the scenarios will include a focus on anti-discriminatory practice and empowerment. This juxtaposition between providing professional support based on experience, knowledge and skills while enabling service users to identify their own individual strengths and solutions ideologically challenges the core purpose of social work in a personalisation context. Given this inherent dilemma, how can social workers and social work students prepare for and improve their practice within a personalisation context?

The key to this may lie in a basic social work skill that is often forgotten or overlooked by the busy professional immersed in the process-driven, performance-managed bureaucracy of their agency – listening.

Instead of using information provided by or about service users to aid the social worker in moving towards a solution, it may be more important and useful to focus on the messages beneath the surface. The skill then becomes learning how to listen and interpret rather than learning how to respond and advise. The remainder of this chapter seeks to embrace this approach. By listening to the experiences of individuals we will begin to appreciate the uniqueness of each scenario and develop skills in responding to the individual rather than the situation or information they provide.

The scenarios come from three individuals who have agreed to share information about their lives with the hope and belief that it will support your learning. The individuals have all been asked the following two questions.

1.   What difference has personalisation made to you?

2.   How can social workers support you in this process?

By using two open-ended questions, it is hoped that the individuals felt able to express the breadth of their experience in a way which they were comfortable with. Atkinson (1998) suggests life-story interviewers need to use an informal approach using open-ended questions which help the person create and convey his or her meaning through the story. This approach also enables the individuals to emphasise key points and highlight the order and importance of any aspects of the process. In this sense the three interviews were semi-structured, allowing the interviewer to ask additional questions or clarification on certain points. Atkinson (1998) stresses the importance of enabling the respondent to maintain control over what goes into the story, how it is said and how it is read at the end. Atkinson asserts that giving less structure to the format of the interview will make this more likely. The interviews were recorded by hand and written up by the interviewer. The individuals were given an opportunity to make any changes before providing final approval of the written narratives. The individuals have chosen to change their names for the purpose of the book.

It must be noted that there is no intention to suggest that the three individuals represent typical experiences in relation to receiving an individual budget. The process therefore is not intended to contribute or add to any valid or reliable primary research in this area. The purpose of the chapter is to provide an opportunity to develop key social work skills, including listening, understanding, interpreting and reflecting. It also encourages an appreciation of the power dynamics that exist between the service user and the professionals. Finally it is hoped that the narratives support students in adopting an anti-discriminatory and anti-oppressive approach to their practice, as discussed in Chapter 2.

ACTIVITY **5.1**

• *In pairs, take it in turns to describe an incident or time in your life that changed you or the way you thought about things. It could be anything from a conversation you had with someone or something major like giving birth or the loss of a loved one. Explain to your partner what happened, how it felt and how it changed your outlook.*

• *Once you have heard the story, ask your partner to summarise their understanding of what this event meant to you. Try to identify any key words the person used and the central meaning or point to the story.*

COMMENT

It would be true to say that we all use stories to describe, define and construct our lives in some way. This may involve recounting a story or anecdote to a friend or reflecting on a longer period of one's life as part of a speech, for example at a wedding, a leaving do or retirement. In each scenario the importance of the story is not only in what happened but the meaning given to it either by the individuals themselves or others hearing the story. We may have been moved by the story in this short activity or struck by the power in this simple exchange of words. The story tells us about the uniqueness of this person yet can be shared and understood by others. A narrative can give a window into the internalised world and suggest how the individual connects with society and culture.

Narrative studies

Before considering the three service user stories, it might be useful to explore the purpose and value of narratives generally. Smith and Sparkes (2008) suggest that we organise our experiences into narratives and assign meaning to them through storytelling. In this way, *narrative helps constitute and construct our realities and modes of being* (p. 2). Because meaning is so basic to human beings, we constantly explore the meanings that make up our own and others' worlds.

Narrative analysis assumes that language conveys meaning and that how the story is told is often more important than what is said (Goodley, 2001). Goodley suggests that narrative allows researchers to explore lived experiences and preserve a sense of the individual. It is important to recognise, however, that narratives are not simply personal but are heavily influenced by the social and cultural contexts in which individuals exist. In this sense the individual understands his or her own world according to his or her past experiences.

In recent years, narrative forms of inquiry have become increasingly visible within disability studies (Goodley et al., 2004; Marks, 1999; Smith and Sparkes, 2005; Thomas, 1999; Todd, 2006). However, this has led to debate concerning the level of emphasis placed on the individual. This viewpoint is largely located within disability studies whereby the fundamental assumption is that disability is *quintessentially collective* (French and Swain, 2006). The Disabled People's Movement insists that disability is experienced through structural, environmental and attitudinal barriers that marginalise, limit and shape people's lives. There is a concern, therefore, that to pay so much attention to the individual experience perpetuates medical-model thinking in that the problem is located with the individual and there is no need therefore for society to adjust. While expressing this concern, Armstrong (2003) suggests there must also be a recognition that to deny the individual experience can equally limit our understandings and that the social model of disability relies on an understanding of both the individual and collective experiences of disablement.

Furthermore, the absence of disabled people's voices from history has increasingly been highlighted. An appreciation of the depth of the prejudice against disabled people is unlikely without a thorough understanding of their history. The documented narratives of institutional living described by Atkinson (2005) evidence the richness of knowledge one can gain from studying the lived experiences from those who have experienced history first hand. Beresford (2003) suggests that the ignorance of researchers leads to them thinking they are better 'knowers' and sources of knowledge than the people who actually experienced it or who witnessed it.

Borsay (2005) suggests that oral history is as much about survival and change as it is to attach meaning. It provides the foundation for collective empowerment and resistance. Oral histories allow us to re-examine and develop new perspectives both ideologically and practically through policy development and practice. Borsay (2005, p. 385) suggests:

> *Oral history can bring about new understandings. It can challenge assumptions, develop a fuller, more rounded and democratic account and may even transform history.*

This is of particular importance when we consider the personalisation agenda. The documentation of the diverse and creative ways that people have personalised their own support provides ideas and support to those considering the path ahead. Sharing and disseminating individual stories have been central to empowering both individuals and professionals to think creatively. The diverse ways individuals have used their budgets have encouraged service users and professionals to think in terms of solutions rather than services.

Finally, oral histories may lead to individual empowerment. Borsay (2005) suggests that telling stories can become *acts of liberation for those whose self esteem has been battered by discrimination* (p. 7). The opportunity to review one's life is important. Finnegan (1992) suggests that the telling of personal narrative can actually help people validate their lives and make sense of their various life experiences.

This brief literature review of the value of oral histories should inform your reading of the following narratives. Clearly it is important to listen to what is being said and by whom, but we must also pay attention to the underlying messages and meanings the three individuals attach to their stories. We will reflect on the storytellers' experiences of actually telling the story and consider whether this has been an empowering or useful exercise for them. Finally, we must remember that stories need to be placed within a social and cultural context. Oliver (2000) suggests insider views, though essential, must be connected to political analysis in order to bring about change. The purpose therefore of using individual stories in this chapter is to read and reflect on the diverse experiences of the individual but then to focus on any common themes in relation to histories of marginalisation, discrimination and oppression. This will provide us with the knowledge to generate and support change in the most useful way.

The service users

Eric

Eric is a 42-year-old man. He lives in his own home and has family close by. Eric has been in his own home for two years, having lived in a residential setting prior to this. Eric describes himself as having high-functioning autism, Asperger's and mental health difficulties. Eric is a very intelligent man. He has attended university and has continued to study in areas such as history, philosophy and archaeology. Eric says he does need support to help him function in life but is clear that the support must be on his terms and he requires others to understand his perspective and mindset in order for it to work successfully.

Eric's story

I have been receiving an individual budget for a year now and I have learnt so much in that time. If I was to go back to the beginning of the year I would have done things differently but I didn't know then what I now know. I don't like the fact that I have to rely on benefits but I guess I also know that doing a job will make me ill. I have lost every job I have done. It's always the same story, I work for three months and at my first appraisal I end up being sacked. This leads to my mental health deteriorating quite rapidly. I have had a number of hospital admissions as a result. My doctor has advised me not to work and that is why I need to use an individual budget to support me at present.

For me the big difference an individual budget has made is that I have more freedom to spend the money on supporting myself in a way that suits me although it's not been easy. Prior to receiving my individual budget I got direct payments but this was difficult as money had to be spent on support hours and although I needed support from other people I also felt I could meet my support needs in other ways if I used the money more flexibly. I was told I could use the money flexibly, but for me I like rules to be clear and I did not feel comfortable spending the money 'outside the rule book'. With an individual budget you are allowed to spend the money more flexibly so it meant I could think about things such as assistive technology and educational support, which have hugely benefited my well-being.

For example, for £300 I was able to go on an organised historical trip with other people for a week. This included accommodation, food and support to visit battlefields with guided tours. The type of support offered was ideal. It took away any worry of making arrangements and decisions, it gave me a break from my routine, it relaxed me as I enjoy educational stimulation and, most importantly, the support was no different from the support anyone else on the trip received. I could not have done this trip alone so it was a perfect option.

One of the things this has taught me is that it is much better to have money from social services with no strings attached. At the beginning, my individual budget was worked out as giving me less money than a direct payment and all I could think was: surely it makes sense to take more money. I wouldn't think that now and I would advise others to avoid making the same mistake. I would take up to 25–30 per cent less money if I knew there were no strings attached.

They give you this money to empower you to go to the market and find the right support but if you can only buy one type of support then it doesn't empower you. An individual budget has helped me discover what works for me and I can't see any other way to move forward to avoid another hospital admission. It just has to be on my terms. I've also learnt that with empowerment comes responsibility. You like the nice bits but it's all the other stuff that comes with it. There are a lot of technicalities and I have often needed more advice and help on how to spend the money. It will empower you but it can be a headache.

One of the problems with the individual budget for me was the support plan. I found this very restricting. I understand that social services need to know how I am going to spend the money and the outcomes I will get but sometimes it's hard to say what outcomes you will achieve until you have achieved them. The other problem for me is that an outcome becomes a target and it puts additional stress on me and makes it less likely for me to achieve it.

For example, one of the ways I used the money was to increase the number of dishes I could cook. This was something I had identified and I was keen to do, but the social worker wanted to quantify how many new dishes I would have learnt to prepare by such a date. This just doesn't work for me. I become focused on the target, which then becomes a source of stress and I avoid preparing new meals in fear of failing to meet the target. If I am left alone to build up my repertoire of new dishes I am actually more likely to achieve the outcome and perhaps even exceed it but I can't feel like it's a test.

I think this can actually be a particular problem for people with mental health problems. I often feel social workers and professionals see me as someone they need to fix. They see the budget as helping me overcome the problems and get better. They see mental ill health as being wrong and something they need to put right. Again this is pressure. The reality is I have mental health problems and while I can be supported to reduce the factors leading up to a breakdown, I can't eliminate this altogether.

If I am seen as having learning difficulty with Asperger's, it's fine for me to be accepted with all the nuances I have. It seems everyone will work around me and do things the way I need them to be done – a bit like 'the customer is always right'. But with mental health I am expected to adapt and change the way I do things to fit in with the norm.

Why if you label me with Asperger's and I say black is white it is OK, but if I have a mental health problem you tell me it's an illusion?

Another problem with individual budgets is how you are seen by others in society. I feel it has alienated me from my friends. I know they see me as having a 'slush fund' and really socialising has stopped since I received the budget. People have been working hard for a crust and I have just been given this sum of money for doing nothing. I know that's what people think.

When I lived in a supported-living flat and my problems were very evident to anyone who met me, it was fine for my friends. They visited me in the flat and they were OK with that. They were paying for me to be disabled and I was clearly disabled. As soon as I started walking around the streets happy-go-lucky, looking as right as rain, that was not OK.

Having the individual budget does also put pressure on me to demonstrate that the money is being well spent and I also feel I should be showing signs of recovery to suggest I am making an effort and using the money well. I used to count up how much money had been spent on me but I stopped once I got to £250,000 as it seemed obscene and what's worse, at that point I was going downhill.

I feel I should contribute to society but often I just don't know how I can do this. I resent not being able to work but I also know the danger to myself and others if I do work. It's all about risk and it's heart-breaking.

I find it hard to say what a social worker can do to help as they work within very restrictive systems. They might have ideas of working with people, working on your behalf but it is always contrary to what their managers are telling them. The framework they operate in is too conservative, negative and restrictive.

On an individual level I think social workers need to take people at face value. Don't assume you know better even if the reality is that you are talking to me at a time when my mental health is poor. You need to get inside and understand me and my way of thinking. It's no good telling me I am paranoid. Think of it in terms of me not understanding the evidence I have been presented with. It's not about colluding with me or agreeing with my statements or thoughts but just trying to share my perspective at that time. Even if you think my point of view is dubious or fanciful, take time to understand the fantasy and then work with it. Once we have this dialogue, trust can build and I will be more receptive to support or thinking about things in a different way.

Social workers need to know what's not going to be changed. The fact that things go wrong for me from time to time can't be changed but we can work on the factors leading up to it so as to reduce the frequency or degree to which it happens.

Follow-up

A few days later Eric was sent a draft of the interview and was asked how he felt about telling me his story. He replied:

> I cannot tell you how encouraged I was after we met. I am moved by
> the simplicity you bring to my words. It is what I'd like to say. You have said what I said
> and it reads to me to mean what I meant. I cannot ask for more.
> You [interviewer] have heard enough to note it down, the product being recognisable
> as what I said and perhaps more importantly what I meant. The expression of
> even difficult things in that way becomes the expression of experience rather than
> depression or moaning about it. Thanks for the opportunity to do it and say what
> effect doing it had. It was very positive. I hope your readers and students will benefit
> from it too.

ACTIVITY **5.2**

1. *Without going back to the narrative, make a list of anything you remember to be important for Eric.*

2. *How do you think Eric can stay in control of his life and become empowered?*

3. *What have been the benefits of an individual budget for Eric?*

4. *What have been the problems associated with an individual budget for Eric?*

5. *What does Eric see as society's perception of him receiving an individual budget? Read the Introduction to Chapter 2 and think about any links with Eric's narrative.*

6. *Why does Eric feel that professionals adopt a medical model when they work with him?*

7. *If you were working with Eric, what would you be thinking about in terms of your approach?*

8. *Eric highlights systems restricting the social work role. How do you think you might address this dilemma if you were working with him?*

9. *Eric talks about the stress an outcome-focused approach puts him under. How might you support Eric to develop and demonstrate outcomes within his support plan? Think about the example of preparing dishes to help you do this.*

10. *In what ways do you think Eric's history and experiences have influenced his life today?*

11. *Do you think the process of telling his story has been an empowering experience for him? If so, how? If not, why not?*

12. *Can you make any links with the theory discussed earlier in the chapter?*

Continued

COMMENT

Hopefully you will have connected with this powerful story told by Eric and have a better understanding of how the uniqueness of his own personal biography has influenced his perspective today. You may have identified some positive ways of working with Eric and, most importantly, I hope the activity will remain with you as you go out into practice and work with individuals and their families.

Andrew

Andrew is a 39-year-old man. He lives in his own home nearby to his family. Andrew has been using an individual budget for the last four years. He uses the money to employ a personal assistant for approximately 30 hours per week to support him in various aspects of daily living. Andrew has been diagnosed with Asperger's and also has cerebral palsy. Andrew lived in a residential home for a number of years until he decided to leave and live independently with support.

Andrew's story

My individual budget has helped me to get my life back. I am now living the life I imagined I would live when I was a teenager. I have my independence. I have my own home under a shared ownership scheme with a housing association. I do what I want to do when I want to do it. There are lots of things that are important to me which I am sure other people don't realise or just take for granted, such as having my own front door key, being able to lock my front door behind me and watching my TV in my lounge rather than quietly upstairs in my room so I don't wake up other residents. I don't have to worry about waking others up.

I don't have to stick to timetables like I did in the residential home. I can have my tea when I want it. I used to have a half-hour slot between 4.45 p.m. and 5.15 p.m. when I had to prepare and cook my tea, eat it and wash up. Now I have meals whenever I want and I do prefer to eat later, like I used to with my family when I was younger. I can use my kitchen whenever I want, which I couldn't do in the residential home. Flexibility – that's the key word. Sometimes I don't have my tea and might just buy something when I am out.

I have recently employed a new personal assistant (PA), which is working out really well. I don't see him as a PA, I see him as a friend. I interviewed and chose him myself and we have lots in common, we are a similar age and I get on well with him. One of the best things about my PA, Bob, is that he had no previous experience in this kind of work so he had no set ideas about supporting people with disabilities. He doesn't know the rule book and he takes his lead from me. He is a father himself and has lots of life experience. I feel comfortable to speak my mind with Bob and we work out his hours to fit both my needs and his family life. We have lots of banter which is good and I have got to know his friends who I play football with every Friday. It's a real mix with men of different ages from early 20s to one player who is 62 years old. They are a good bunch of men who have welcomed me into their group. They even helped my Nan put up a new unit when she moved house.

I've never really had friends or anyone to say *do you want to come to the pub, Andrew?* I now know a group of men who all know my name, there's lots of banter and they treat me like one of the lads. I go out for a drink with them sometimes after football and we are going out for a meal together the week before my birthday next month.

I also use my budget to pay for an IT expert, Tom, to help me with my computer. It's really important that my computer works and I get stressed if I can't use it. I have developed a good friendship with Tom and he helps me with other gadgets and DIY jobs around the house. He also stepped in to support me when my PA wasn't available for a couple of weeks. Tom has also helped me to put something back into my community. He has helped me develop a PowerPoint presentation about my individual budget which I share with others at conferences. I think it is important that I am able to contribute in this way although I am taking a break from it for a while as it can be stressful and time-consuming.

There are some things that are hard with an individual budget. I often feel there is a lot of prejudice about people being given money to spend on meeting their own needs. I think lots of people using individual budgets feel they have to justify how they are spending the money. I think it's working well for me but I also think I am in a minority. It can also be hard to find a PA. I had to do lots of interviews and even if you get a PA who is a 100 per cent match, you may still have a problem with the service provider they work for. It's sometimes hard to work out the boundaries with a PA. They spend so much time with you in your own home and you get to know them well. Sometimes this leads to staff becoming institutionalised even when there are just two of you. It's important to feel comfortable with each other but you have to also feel you are directing the support and making the choices about what you want to do and how you want to be supported. I'm lucky because I have a good PA and I also have family to keep an eye out and help me manage the support but I do worry that if you don't get the right person and you are vulnerable and without family and friends to support you, it could go very wrong.

I don't have that much contact with my social worker as my mum helps me sort out the individual budget. I used to have weekly contact with the social worker when I was living in the residential home and it was very stressful for me and my mum. The social worker also came when there was a crisis and this happened on a regular basis.

I think it is important that social workers are honest and open. They need to be able to listen – and I mean really listen. It's important that they write down your wishes and don't just listen to what you say and then go away and do something different. I have spoken to lots of social workers at conferences and they are often very blinkered and seem a bit institutionalised. I think lots of social workers start off thinking they want to change things but then get locked into the system that doesn't let them have much freedom to do things differently.

I also think service providers find it hard to do things differently. I have met lots of individuals from service provider agencies who want to change things and tailor support to the individual but I don't believe I will see a service provider in my lifetime that can do this. They often talk the talk but then managers want them to do things a certain way and they get used to working within a system.

ACTIVITY **5.3**

1. *Without going back to the narrative, make a list of anything you remember to be important for Andrew.*

2. *Try to identify some of the ways Andrew's individual budget has enabled him to become more included within his community.*

3. *Make a list of the benefits and drawbacks of receiving an individual budget from Andrew's perspective.*

4. *Andrew talks about professional boundaries and the danger of staff becoming institutionalised when working in this way. What do you think Andrew means by this?*

5. *What does Andrew value in a social worker?*

6. *What challenges does Andrew think social workers face?*

7. *Why might Andrew think that he will never see a service provider in his life that can tailor support to the individual's needs?*

8. *Do you think the process of telling his story has been an empowering experience for Andrew? If so, how? If not, why not?*

9. *Can you make any links with the theory discussed earlier in the chapter?*

COMMENT

The activity should have helped you to think about some of the challenges individuals face when directing their own support. Andrew's story tells us of the positive and negative aspects. Like Eric, Andrew also talks about the prejudice individuals face in using individual budgets. As social workers it is important to recognise and acknowledge the emotional impact this process has on individuals and to support them in working through these issues.

Elizabeth (Andrew's mum)

Andrew's individual budget has been life-changing. When he was in the residential home I was in constant fear for his life. The anguish and pain of seeing your loved one suffer and not knowing what to do to make it better is terrible. It wasn't the answer to just bring him back home as this would not have given him the independence he so much strived for. He would not have the quality of life or reached his potential, as he now has. When Andrew moved into the home, we were assured that this was a move to help him become more independent and the next step would be his own home. Andrew had really wanted more independence and was troubled by his inability to get this prior to moving into the residential home. I worried about every phone call and I could not believe the decline I saw in Andrew in such a short space of time. Towards the end of his time in the residential home, Andrew was heavily medicated, had put on a lot of weight and was a shadow of his former self. When I look at him today I can hardly believe the difference.

During his time in the residential home, I had often thought how I could use the money spent on him in the home to plan a better life for him living independently but just assumed this was not possible within the rules. Then I read a book by Simon Duffy called *Keys to citizenship.* I couldn't believe I was reading something that I had thought about and I was convinced this would be right for Andrew. I took the book to social services and waved it in front of them as I knew they wouldn't believe me.

At first I felt like I did a lot of shouting and had to make people listen but we did have a good social worker who listened to our side of the story and eventually saw that the residential home was not right for Andrew. The social worker learnt with us about individual budgets and a pilot scheme allowed us to eventually set one up. Once the light went on for us as a family, as well as the social worker, he was brilliant and I really believe he felt proud of what he helped us achieve. He did things that had not been done before, and helped Andrew individually and imaginatively, always taking the lead from Andrew. It certainly was a steep learning curve for both him and ourselves but it was worth it.

Andrew is back to himself, absolutely himself. He is happy, he's getting pleasure from life and he's at peace. He has fun in life and also contributes to society in telling his story and helping to train staff. I still get a kick out of seeing how well he is doing. I often go home and tell my husband something he has achieved and I can't quite believe it when I think back to the days in the residential home. I would never have believed Andrew could be living the life he lives today. He is in good physical shape and is on no medication. He has no issues with obsessive-compulsive disorders which were a real problem for him.

I really believe that it was purely the environment that led to Andrew's decline. When you take away a person's life so they have no control over it, no say in what happens, they become so isolated. It's like torture. Andrew had no reason for living. Everything was controlled and we just couldn't see a way out. He had so many labels attributed to him such as 'high complex needs', 'difficult to handle' and 'attention-seeking', none of which are the real Andrew. Now he is just Andrew. And he has got rid of the labels.

Social workers really need to listen to individuals. They mustn't arrive with their own agenda with what's going on in the office. They need to put the person in the centre. Social workers must believe in themselves and stand firm in their beliefs and values. They must not be swayed by other agendas such as management issues and resource issues. Once they start doing this, they lose sight of the person being at the centre. They need to dig their heels in and stand firm. They should think about the individual as if they were their own. That doesn't mean crossing boundaries or becoming unprofessional, but just adopting the mindset, 'would this be OK for my grandmother?'

Looking back on Andrew's life it is like watching a picture or a film and seeing how things have evolved. We have come a long way and it's been a steep learning curve but I feel we have achieved change for Andrew and for others, which does give some satisfaction. Looking back now and talking about it again makes me realise just how far he has come and how brilliantly well he is doing.

ACTIVITY 5.4

1. Without going back to the narrative, make a list of some of the words Elizabeth used to describe the transition Andrew has made.

2. Elizabeth describes putting trust in professionals who had suggested residential care would be right for her son. How do you think this made her feel towards those professionals when she saw Andrew's decline?

3. What factors did Elizabeth attribute to her son's decline?

4. What challenges did Elizabeth face when trying to get the best for her son?

5. Elizabeth describes the constant use of negative labels. How do you think this impacted on Andrew and his family?

6. In what ways does Elizabeth believe social workers can support individuals and their families?

7. Do you think the process of telling her story has been an empowering experience? If so, how? If not, why not?

8. Can you make any links with the theory discussed earlier in the chapter?

COMMENT

This activity demonstrates the impact on the wider family. Elizabeth describes her frustration and clearly felt her views and ideas would not be valued. It is interesting to note that she had a clear vision for Andrew but felt unable to convey this to the professionals until she had a book to prove it. As social workers it is important to remember that expertise can often be found within the individual and their family. The role of the social worker is to help release the imagination that individuals have and value their contribution. It is also interesting to note that although Elizabeth was always willing to work with professionals, she often felt she needed to be very assertive and forthright in getting the best support for her son.

ACTIVITY 5.5

Hopefully the three narratives have helped you to think about some of the benefits and drawbacks of receiving an individual budget. You may also have made some links with the theory both in this chapter and in Chapter 2. To help you reflect on these narratives think about and discuss with others the following questions.

1. Were there any similarities in the experiences or viewpoints for the three individuals? If so, what were they and why do you think these were shared values?

2. Were there any differences in the three narratives? If so, what were they and why might there have been diversity in their values or perspectives?

3. In what ways might narratives help you develop good practice within social work?

Continued

COMMENT

Narratives give us some additional insight into the internal worlds of others. The three individuals describe experiences and events which have shaped their lives. They have also attached meaning to those experiences which help us understand how they relate to society, and in this case professionals. Their past experiences and histories have clearly influenced their interpretation of events and in both cases the experience of making a transition from residential care to independent living and gaining control in their lives is a shared value upon which they all place great importance. There are many differences in the way Eric and Andrew have designed and directed the support in their life and they differ in the emphasis they place on certain aspects. For example, Eric describes the process of support planning and needing to be in complete control as crucially important, whereas Andrew emphasises the importance of relationships and extending social networks as centrally important.

All three value social workers who can listen and try to understand their perspective. They also share in their belief that social workers have to be strong and committed to work within very challenging and restrictive organisations.

RESEARCH SUMMARY

The Shaping Our Lives, National User Network published a literature-informed discussion paper in 2007. Lead author Peter Beresford used the paper to highlight the experience and views of service users and carers as part of the wider national review of social work practice in England. In light of major policy changes and direction in social work including the person-alisation agenda, the research focused on the activities and tasks social workers engage in and the approach and qualities social workers possess. The following findings emerged.

- *Service users placed a particular value on the social work relationship and positive personal qualities such as warmth, respect, being non-judgemental, listening, treating people equally, being trustworthy, openness and honesty, reliability and communicating well.*

- *Service users value social work practitioners who:*
  - *support them to work out their own agendas with them;*
  - *give them time to sort things out;*
  - *are available and accessible;*
  - *provide continuity of support;*
  - *are reliable and deliver;*
  - *are responsive;*
  - *have a good level of knowledge and expertise;*
  - *value the expertise of the service user.*

In relation to self-directed support, service users and carers reported traditional profes-sional approaches to assessment as being particularly unhelpful. Service users wanted to see social workers drawing on principles of independent living and rights based approaches in supporting them to make their own self assessment.

Continued

91

CHAPTER SUMMARY

This chapter has provided an insight into the experiences of three individuals directing their own support. While these experiences cannot be generalised, they offer a chance to consider the potential opportunities and barriers involved in supporting people to direct their own support. The narratives encourage the reader to develop reflective practice by taking time to listen to and understand service users' perceptions of events and experiences. Practitioners can support service users to identify their own solutions rather than being too quick to jump in with standard service responses. The chapter has helped you to make important links between theoretical perspectives and practice. The chapter has encouraged the reader to consider the ethical principles and dilemmas involved in balancing the importance of the individual perspective versus the collective experience of disability.

It would appear from both the narratives and the research findings above, that while roles, tasks and approaches are changing, service users and carers remain unchanged in their expectation that personal qualities such as warmth, respect and openness are integral to all social work practice.

FURTHER READING

Atkinson, D (2004) Research and empowerment: Involving people with learning difficulties in oral and life history research. *Disability and Society*, 19 (7), December: 691–703.

This article draws from two oral and life-history projects to explore the multiple uses of storytelling. It focuses on learning disability and the reader is encouraged to develop insight into the meaning of people's past experiences.

Atkinson, D (2005) Narratives and people with learning disabilities. In Grant, G, Goward, P, Richardson, M and Ramcharan, P (2005) *Learning disability. A life cycle approach to valuing people.* Berkshire: Open University Press. Chapter 1, p.s 7–27.

This chapter provides a number of narratives from people with learning disabilities who have lived in institutional settings. The reader is encouraged to understand their histories and transitions following the closure of such institutions, exploring how they adapted to living in the community.

WEBSITE

www.scie.org.uk/socialcaretv

You can watch a number of videos documenting personal stories from individuals who are directing their own support. The series covers a range of service user groups and settings.

Chapter 6

Balancing rights and risks in self-directed support

ACHIEVING A SOCIAL WORK DEGREE

This chapter will begin to help you meet the following National Occupational Standards.
Key role 1: Prepare for, and work with individuals, families, carers, groups and communities to assess their needs and circumstances.
- Work with individuals, families and carers, groups and communities to enable them to assess and make informed decisions about their needs, circumstances, risks, preferred options and resources.
- Assess needs, risks and options taking into account legal and other requirements.

Key role 4: Assess and manage risks to individuals, families and carers, groups and communities.
- Identify and assess the nature of risk.
- Balance the rights and responsibilities of individuals, families, carers, groups and communities with associated risk.
- Regularly monitor, re-assess, manage risk to individuals, families, carers, groups and communities.
- Work within the risk assessment and management procedures of your own and other relevant organisations and professions.

Also important here are the General Social Care Council Codes of practice for social care employers (GSCC, 2002), which state the following.
Social care workers must protect the rights and promote the interests of service users and carers; this includes:
- Treating each person as an individual (1.1).
- Respecting and, where appropriate, promoting the individual views and wishes of both service users and carers (1.2).
- Supporting service users' rights to control their lives and make informed choices about the services they receive (1.3).

As a social care worker, you must promote the independence of service users while protecting them as far as possible from danger or harm.
- Promoting the independence of service users and assisting them to understand and exercise their rights (3.1).
- Recognising and using responsibly the power that comes from your work with service users and carers (3.8).

The chapter will also introduce you to the following academic standards as set out in the 2008 social work subject benchmark statement.

Defining principles
4.6
4.7

Introduction

In this chapter we will consider one of the most contested issues surrounding the personalisation agenda. While most practitioners, managers, policy-makers and academics would share the view that a 'good life' is one that requires a balance between freedom and control, the definition of a 'right balance' and the means of achieving that balance vary considerably. In this chapter we will trace the policy/legislative development as well as ideologies, theories and research that have influenced the safeguarding agenda. This chapter will facilitate the reader to critically reflect on the challenges practitioners face in supporting individuals to direct their own support in a way which balances choice and safety.

ACTIVITY 6.1

- *Think about some of the risks you take in your own life. This might be something simple such as walking home late at night alone or excessive drinking, smoking or perhaps motorcycle racing. Make two lists, the first noting the benefits involved in taking the risk and the other noting the dangers associated with this activity.*

- *Now imagine that a close family member or friend has been asked to carry out a risk assessment to decide whether you should be allowed to carry out this behaviour. Do you think they would have similar lists? Do you think they would agree to the risk?*

COMMENT

The point to this exercise is to demonstrate the individual nature of choice and risk. Unless we have an appreciation of our own freedom of choice in relation to risk, we will not be able to support service users effectively. Risk-taking is a unique experience. For one person a parachute jump may be a risk too far; for someone else it could be their job. Your experience, age, upbringing, strengths, financial situation, health status, fears and previous experiences will all influence how you balance risk and choice. In choosing a family member or friend to carry out a risk assessment, you may have come up with a different list from your own and the balance between the choice and the risk may also have been different.

Risk-taking is part of our daily routine and perhaps something we are unaware of. It might be crossing the road at a dangerous spot or taking a short-cut alone at night. We may not necessarily think of these aspects of daily life as being risky or potentially dangerous and we certainly don't need signed approval before we make such decisions. In this sense we have the freedom to make choices that could present an element of risk and which we may on reflection consider as an error of judgement. The difference for service users, however, is that they often do not have complete freedom or power to make decisions about major and minor aspects of daily living. The fact that a service or money is being provided by the public purse gives professionals a level of power to influence or control the decisions that service users make. Often masked by health and safety regulations within a risk-averse context, professionals routinely impose organisational as well as their personal values in relation to risk.

ACTIVITY **6.2**

Try to identify an occasion when you have been formally assessed. It may have been a medical issue, a mortgage application, a driving test or an interview. How did it feel?

- *Did you have any control?*

- *Could you influence the decision? If not why?*

- *How did you behave?*

- *Would you have gained a better outcome if you had been more fully involved with the decision?*

COMMENT

As professionals we need to acknowledge what happens when we assess service users. We need to think about the power we hold and assert either knowingly or otherwise. We need to acknowledge that although we have some expertise in making assessments in this area, the real expertise lies with the person. Even your involvement in a medical assessment could affect the outcome. You may not have the expertise to finalise the diagnosis but the information you give, the way you are treated by the doctor and the way you behave may all influence the doctor's judgement in relation to diagnosis and treatment. Supporting individuals to make informed decisions in relation to risk is very difficult. As professionals we do not want to collude with decisions that make somebody unsafe but we do need to consider fully the opportunities that will arise for each individual in taking any risk.

Policy backdrop

Over the last decade, concepts of risk, choice, protection, abuse, vulnerability and safeguarding have dominated adult social care and social work. Service user voice, practice and research have influenced policy development and direction considerably. In order to fully appreciate current thinking and practice it will be useful to take some time to reflect on these changes.

No secrets

The Department of Health guidance, *No secrets: Guidance on developing and implementing multi-agency policies and procedures to protect vulnerable adults from abuse* (2000), aimed to provide a framework for professionals to work within to protect vulnerable adults from abuse. *No secrets* recognised that some forms of abuse were criminal offences and that police investigations were required and appropriate. The guidance was the first formal government recognition of adult protection as a public duty requiring formal co-operation of many agencies. It was viewed as a groundbreaking step in acknowledging public responsibility for an issue that had been hidden and invisible for a long time.

The guidance, although issued in 2000 under section 7 of the Local Authority and Social Services Act 1970, does not carry the same status as legislation. Its compliance is assessed as part of a statutory inspection process but with 'good reason' a local authority can ignore such guidance. The other limiting factor is that no other agencies are influenced by section 7 and its ability therefore to adequately protect vulnerable adults has been widely criticised. In reality, local authorities reported difficulties in developing robust partnership procedures with key stakeholders and enforcing clear mandates for dealing with reports and incidents of abuse (DH, 2008g). The guidance, however, provided useful definitions and practice guidance including the development of multi-disciplinary frameworks to support working with key partners including the police and health professionals in addressing issues of abuse.

Care Standards Act 2000

The main aim of the Act was to reform the regulatory system for care services in England and Wales. The Act established a new, independent regulatory body, the National Care Standards Commission, for social care and private and voluntary health care services in England, with an arm of the National Assembly for Wales carrying out a similar function. The Act provides for the regulation of the social care workforce through the introduction of a registration system for social workers via the establishment of the General Social Care Council (GSCC) and in relation to adults the introduction of the Protection of Vulnerable Adults list (POVA), which acts as a workforce ban. The list came into operation in 2004 and stated that staff who work in social care domiciliary or registered home settings providing care can be referred to the list if they abuse, neglect or place adults at risk. It is also a criminal offence to apply to do any work with a vulnerable adult while on the list. One of the current concerns is that as people purchase services and support that do not come under the regulated services as defined by the Care Standards Act 2000, they may not benefit from the same protection.

Criminal Records Bureau (CRB) (2002)

The CRB, an executive agency of the Home Office, was established under Part V of the Police Act 1997 and launched in March 2002 following public concern about the safety of children, young people and vulnerable adults. One of the main reasons for establishing the CRB was to reduce the number of organisations being sued for employing convicted criminals who then went on to abuse vulnerable people while in the course of their employment. Arguably, the impetus for the development of this agency explains its inherent weakness in that a CRB check only provides a snapshot of an individual's suitability to work with vulnerable people. It only informs an employer of past convictions and has no real currency from any time after the check is completed. In relation to personalisation, CRB checks have been a source of contention, with no standardised national practice whether a CRB is required for individuals using personal/individual budgets.

Sexual Offences Act 2003

Before this piece of legislation, there had only been a small number of prosecutions for sexual offences against people with learning disabilities. The Act, which used the Mental

Health Act 1983 definition of 'mental disorder', included people with a learning disability. The Act made it illegal for a person to engage in sexual activity with someone who could not legally consent to that sexual activity. The Act also set clear parameters for those working with individuals with a mental disorder, stating that any sexual activity between a care worker and a person with a mental disorder is prohibited while the relationship of care continues. The wording of this Act is such that it would include those employed as personal assistants or providing support purchased as part of a personal/individual budget.

Mental Capacity Act 2005

The Mental Capacity Act importantly stressed the guiding principle 'to assume capacity' in all situations. As a starting point professionals are to assume the person has the capacity to make a decision. In this sense it is the role of the professional to prove where capacity does not exist rather than the individual having to prove they do have capacity. This was an important shift and has been used to guard against blanket decisions being taken in regard to people perceived to be lacking capacity. The introduction of the Mental Capacity Act also shifted the balance in relation to notions of risk assessments, which had often been viewed as a professional activity that solely depended on the expertise of the professional. It could be argued that this piece of legislation has forced professionals to work in a more inclusive, person-centred manner which takes account of the service user's wishes and perceptions of balancing risk and choice. The Act, however, does reinforce a clear role for professionals in supporting individuals to make decisions. Under section 44 of the Act it is a criminal offence to *wilfully neglect or deliberately ill treat a person who lacks capacity*.

Included within this Act was the establishment of the 'best-interest' decision-making process. Once a person has been assessed as lacking capacity to make a particular decision at that time, the Best Interest Checklist provides a framework to ensure a person still remains central to this process. The checklist considers a number of aspects including whether the person is likely to regain capacity, how the person can be fully involved in the process, the person's past and present wishes, feelings, beliefs and values along with the views of those close to that individual where appropriate.

Safeguarding Vulnerable Groups Act 2006

This Act came into force in November 2006, heralding significant changes in the way people who work with children and vulnerable adults are vetted. In relation to adults, key features of the Act include the continuation of a list barring unsuitable individuals from working with vulnerable people. The Independent Safeguarding Authority (ISA) established as part of this Act will make decisions about which individuals should be barred. One of the key differences to previous checks under the CRB system is that the ISA will be able to respond to changes to a person's suitability. When new information such as a conviction or a caution or a referral from an employer becomes known about an individual already registered with the ISA, the Authority will review its original decision to bar. This is not available as part of the CRB process. It is important to note, at the time of writing, that the implementation of the Vetting and Barring scheme was halted by the coalition government in 2010. The coalition government stated that it intended to *review the criminal records and vetting and barring regime and scale it back to common sense levels* (HM Government, 2010, p. 20).

Independence, choice and risk: A framework for supported decision making

The Department of Health prepared a best-practice guide (Department of Health, 2007b) on dealing with risk in health and social care. The guide provides a common set of principles with the aim that individuals and organisations would use them as a basis to support people to make decisions about their own lives and manage any risks in relation to those choices. The governing principle suggests that people have the right to live their lives to the full as long as that does not stop others from doing the same. Professionals need to work in a way that takes account of the benefits in terms of independence, well-being and choice as well as potential risks to the individual and/or others. A supported decision-making tool was provided with the guide designed to support and record the discussion when a person's choices involve an element of risk. Based on person-centred principles of inclusion and self determinism, the tool enables the person to express their wishes and perceptions in relation to both choice and risk. It also encourages the individual to identify solutions to enhance safety and minimise risk while ensuring choice and opportunities remain central to the process. The guide finally works towards the development of an action plan, noting any decisions, disagreements and a clear framework for monitoring and reviewing the plan (DH, 2007b).

ACTIVITY 6.3

Read Annex A of the Independence, choice and risk *guide on the Department of Health website* (www.dh.gov.uk)*. Study the tool and consider the following.*

* *Do you think the tool balances risk and choice?*

* *If so, how? If not, why not?*

* *How could you as a practitioner support somebody to work through this tool?*

* *In what ways do you think the tool reflects social model thinking and a person-centred approach?*

COMMENT

You may have had a service user in mind as you approached this exercise. You may have found that the tool was helpful in that it focused as much on the individual's wants and choices as it did on potential risks and needs. Often in social work we are encouraged to concentrate solely on needs and risks; required paperwork can make assessments quite rigid and restrictive. If we are able to support individuals to begin with by identifying what they want in a certain situation, it can be easier then to identify and assess their needs and risks and, more importantly, the solutions that might be available to address them. In many ways this does reflect social-model thinking, acknowledging individuals with strengths and expertise in their own lives. It seeks to remove external barriers which may be preventing them from pursuing choices that are important to them rather than stopping the person from taking the risk because of the existence of the external barrier. The case study below may help to demonstrate this point.

Jude is a 25-year-old woman with a learning disability and mental health difficulties. She lives in her own home and chooses to be supported by a personal assistant. In eight months Jude has worked through four personal assistants (PAs), each of whom has left after a short period. Jude's mum and her social worker are now very concerned that this arrangement is not working for Jude and it is placing her at increased risk. Initially Jude was determined that she would interview and recruit the personal assistant on her own. She said that she was sick of staff being chosen for her and, now that she has an individual budget, it is her choice. The supported decision tool was used to work through what Jude wanted to help her reflect on past experiences and to identify any potential risks. Jude attributed the high turnover of staff to changes in her PAs' personal circumstances. At the end of the process, the social worker formally expressed her disagreement with Jude. She suggested that Jude was not choosing the right staff to support her and, therefore, the arrangement was more likely to break down. The social worker suggested that Jude might access some independent support to help her recruit a new PA. Reluctantly Jude agreed to this and employed a user-led organisation to build up a job description and person specification. She was supported to interview the candidates and talk through her perceptions of the staff. Jude employed two PAs, which she admits she would never have chosen in the past. Jude likes both of the PAs, who are very different from herself and from each other. Jude has now had the same two PAs for over a year.

Putting People First concordat

As well as the objectives of placing social inclusion at the heart of modern government, there was also recognition that this would mean service users would increasingly access universal services. This raised questions for those leading the transformation about the additional mechanisms that may be required to be put in place to ensure safeguarding issues were adequately considered. The concordat identified the need to review legislation and policy relating to safeguarding to ensure that all policies were heading in the same direction (DH, 2007a).

In response to this measure and in recognition of the growing number of service users purchasing services from unregulated agencies and individuals, Adult Directors of Adult Social Services (ADASS) developed a seven-part plan that would essentially call for adult protection legislation. The focus of this plan was to ensure that the new freedoms to commission individual care and support would be protected by effective legal safeguards. While ADASS recognised that individuals would have the same recourse as other citizens to wider protection agencies such as Trading Standards, the Ombudsmen and complaints systems, they also acknowledged the importance of effective advocacy and good risk assessment and management within this context (ADASS, 2008). It will be useful to spend some time studying the specific legislative recommendations suggested by ADASS, which call for more invasive measures in dealing with suspected abuse. In addition, a consultation process (DH, 2008g) designed to be part of the review of the *No secrets* (2000) guidance found a clear message emerging that there was a need for a more integrated safeguarding framework which would have to widen to include both regulated and non-regulated care.

Policy summary

This policy backdrop provides us with an appreciation of the journey social work has undertaken in relation to notions of risk, abuse, vulnerability, safeguarding and independence. The current government has continued to grapple with and balance a moral duty to care and intervene with a reluctance to legislate and control the lives of adults. In the past such considerations were rarely given to vulnerable adults, who were perceived and treated as passive recipients of care. The rise and power of the collective voice of disabled people has shifted the balance in the relationship between the state and the individual, questioning the paternalistic nature of welfare. The introduction of personalisation has further questioned these concepts and relationships. It is perhaps no surprise that social workers question their role as they are faced, on the one hand, by policy calling for the promotion of service user choice and control and, on the other hand, notions of accountability and risk management dominate their day-to-day practice.

As the policy backdrop suggests, the discourse surrounding safeguarding and personalisation is far from harmonious and, in the next part of the chapter, we will explore the opportunities and barriers in relation to these two agendas. Given the current climate within which practitioners operate, coupled with an ever-increasing risk-averse culture emerging in the UK, many social workers and organisations have been somewhat nervous of an agenda which appears to be driven by a single-minded approach towards self-directed support. Champions of safeguarding fear that those pressing for personalisation are *ignoring the potential risks, especially abuse in applying personalisation willy-nilly* (Macintyre and Washington 2009). A key concern for some Unison members is that personalisation is being universally applied to all individuals and service user groups and while it will work for some, others need good, reliable care, not cash (Unison Eastern, 2009). Similarly, the chief executive of Action on Elder Abuse, Gary Fitzgerald (Lombard, 2010), claims that the government is taking the perspective of adult physical disability and applying it without any consideration across the board to people who are in highly vulnerable situations. Fitzgerald, along with others both in practice and in policy, is sceptical of improved outcomes being achieved for older people through personalisation, sensing that it could actually put them at more risk. Henwood and Hudson (2007) in their study found that some professional staff had concerns whether older people can cope with the demands of self-directed support. Interestingly, a survey carried out by Community Care 2008, in which 600 social workers responded, found that only 11 per cent viewed the plan to extend personalisation to all users as appropriate, while 96 per cent of local authority staff feared it would risk making users more vulnerable (Community Care, 2008). It is important to note, however, that only 22 per cent of the respondents felt well-informed about individual budgets and 19 per cent about self-directed support. This was also found to be the case in Henwood and Hudson's 2007 study in which those expressing concerns about implementation also demonstrated a poor understanding of the different forms personalisation could take and showed a lack of appreciation of the contribution of support brokerage for service users.

A major concern for those sceptical of the safety offered within personalised support is the lack of regulation. As vast numbers of vulnerable individuals engage with unregulated agencies and individuals, the likelihood of risk will increase significantly and, as one listener commented on the Radio 5 *Cash for care* debate, a *Granny P tragedy is waiting to happen* (Macintyre and Washington, 2009). Further caution emerged from research carried out by Manthorpe et al. (2009). As part of the wider national evaluation of individual budgets, adult protection leads in the 13 individual budget pilot sites were interviewed, focusing on risk and policy congruence between potentially competing agendas of choice and control and of protection and harm reduction. Some of the areas of concern raised in this study included potential for financial abuse, particularly for older people both in terms of family arrangements and dealing with outside agencies. Respondents also highlighted the potential risks associated with the breadth of services and support that can be purchased with an individual budget as opposed to those directly commissioned by the social worker. While workers supported the ability for service users to exercise choice and purchase services from an open market, they were concerned about the lack of regulation and potential for exploitative practices being established. Respondents reported frequent dilemmas in practice in wanting to offer choice and independence while promoting well-being and ensuring safety of service users. One respondent commented:

> I'm stressed between my social work role – giving people independence, choice and control – and people being more prone to abuse because people don't take out CRB checks and we don't as an authority do CRB checks for service users while some do.

> (Manthorpe et al., 2009, p. 1473)

In addition, concern was expressed in relation to the 'wrong' people responding to advertisements seeking personal support. As service users are encouraged to be creative and use regular community facilities such as local shops and newspapers to recruit personal assistants, without a regulated procedure, service users could be placed at further risk. Some respondents also highlighted the danger of families seeing relatives receiving substantial incomes each week, offering help and giving a very low return for the payments. The blurring of boundaries was also highlighted as an area of concern both within families as described above but also as intensive working relationships between the service user and the personal assistant are established.

RESEARCH SUMMARY

Research carried out by Flynn (2006) looking at the developing role of personal assistants found the serious downsides of direct payments included: broken trust, dishonesty, discourtesy, incompetence and abuse, including physical, sexual, psychological and financial. Out of the 16 people interviewed in this study, half the people getting direct payments described abuse they or their loved ones had experienced. Some of the quotations included the following.

> Even though I can say what I want, it's scary to think what it's like for people who are totally dependent. They'd be walked all over given half a chance. (p. 37)

> There have been those who bring their kids to play while they work. (p. 37)

Continued

They get up earlier than me so they can have a bit of time to themselves, read my paper or magazines and they might note things down on my paper – little things. *(p. 37)*

I've had two alcoholics and people who've taken my money – the lot. (p. 39)

Another used to pretend to walk the dog and she'd be sitting at the end of the road having a fag. It's not good enough. *(p. 39)*

Flynn (2006) found that individuals set up their own safeguards, including only employing people they knew well and trusted or being around when PAs were present. Interestingly the research revealed that no formal alerts had been made and no complaints or adult protection procedures had been invoked.

At a wider level, some respondents commented on the potential for people to become isolated and that the power of the collective voice on commissioning, developing and regulating may be lost. The potential dangers of fragmenting services and support in this way have been well documented in the literature relating to direct payments (see Spandler, 2004). Henwood and Hudson (2007) found that one of the ideological obstacles to the paradigm of self-directed support was the loss of collectivism. In their study they identified an apparent tension between the emphasis on the individual and the collective objectives. The two quotations below highlight this perception.

CSCI (Commission Social Care Inspection) are trying to connect us to quality of life outcomes for people but individual budgets are potentially disconnecting us from it … community regeneration initiatives are based on areas not individuals.

(head of service, p. 21)

My son is out constantly but sometimes he would just like to be in a group activity rather than on his own with his carer. I like direct payments and individual budgets and they are working well for us but I do think it isolates him.

(carer, p. 21)

The concern in relation to safeguarding is the fear that, as services fragment and people become more isolated, this may give rise to more exploitative practices by individuals, their families or smaller agencies. In their study, Henwood and Hudson (2007) found that the decision to move ahead in developing self-directed support required careful risk assessment and contingency planning. All case study sites interviewed recognised the potential risk to personal safety and expressed some uncertainty in balancing the responsibility to support people to take greater individual responsibility while being careful not to neglect their own professional responsibility to ensure the service users were safe in doing so.

Many of the perceived risks in relation to personalisation relate primarily to the concern for the personal safety of the individual and protecting them from external exploitative or abusive practices. It is important to note that financial risk to the local authority and the public purse is also highlighted as a risk in pursuing self-directed support. In Chapter 2, we explored the public perception of providing cash for care. In Chapter 5, in their narratives, both Vince and Andrew commented on how public perception had impacted on their experiences in quite a negative way. Henwood and Hudson (2007) similarly found widespread evidence of explicit and implicit mistrust of service users and a suspicion that people will seek to get as much out of the system as they can. One service manager commented:

> *There has definitely been some abuse of direct payments, we have some people who have crazy packages like holidays to Goa and assistance to night clubs seven nights a week. There are some real horror stories.*
>
> (service manager, p. 23)

> *There is always fear of a small population who may say thank you very much and want something totally different with their money. But then we will end up back at square one when they are knocking on the door again saying I've spent the money but I still have the problem. And where do we stand then?*
>
> (service manager, p. 23)

Not all respondents, however, shared the same sense of mistrust or caution. One project manager commented:

> *People in the system at all levels have philosophical problems. Users could have a subscription to Sky TV or if they are lonely they could use internet dating, these are things that social care money could be legitimately used for. People are not used to coping with these kinds of ideas.*
>
> (project manager, p. 37)

REFLECTION POINT

It is important to note that the research carried out by Henwood and Hudson (2007) was a qualitative piece of research examining the progress of self-directed support in three different localities representing the different points of continuum in relation to progress so far on this agenda.

- *Site 1 was an individual budget pilot site and In Control site and therefore well ahead with the implementation of self-directed support.*

- *Site 2 was described as being ambitious in moving towards comprehensive transformation.*

- *Site 3 had little engagement with the personalisation agenda but had started some small-scale activity in relation to self-directed support.*

It is important to reflect on the methodology used in all research when considering the findings. The purpose and aim of the study, along with issues such as sampling, validity and reliability, are important factors in drawing any conclusions or developing recommendations. I would therefore suggest that you take time to read this interesting and accessible piece of research, which can be accessed free of charge on the internet.

At the beginning of the chapter I commented on the contentious nature surrounding any discourse relating to personalisation and safeguarding. At times it would seem that social workers, managers, policy-makers and academics have positioned themselves in one of the two camps: the 'safeguarders' or the 'personalisers', and that movement between the two is prohibited. While this is not entirely true, there is a definite ideological polarisation in this debate. As with any new policy direction, there will be differences of opinion in relation to ideology and implementation. Duffy and Gillespie (2009) suggest that *the simplest confusion comes by treating personalisation as if it is simply about freedom and treating safeguarding as if it is simply about control* (p. 3). They go on to say that personalisation is not about maximising control but is primarily concerned with designing support so that it is personal, which means they need to fit the person and be suitable for them. Furthermore, Duffy and Gillespie claim that one of the things you can personalise is control itself and that this is sometimes the key to excellent support.

NCIL (1999) suggest that protection from abuse is linked to empowerment and that the more control disabled people have in their lives, the less likely they are to find themselves in abusive situations. They suggest that historically safety has regularly been used as an excuse to deny or curtail disabled people's choice and control and that they should have the same rights to take risks as all citizens.

Before looking at the ways in which personalisation may be able to keep people safer, it will be useful to reflect on traditional services which adult service users access. As Glasby and Littlechild (2009, p. 164) suggest, *new ways of working are often subject to greater scrutiny than current approaches, with the result that we criticise the new without really subjecting the old to the same standards.*

ACTIVITY 6.4

Read the following statements taken from a report compiled by In Control *in 2009. After each statement, tick to say whether you agree, disagree or don't know.*

- *People are safer when they are in congregate or institutional environments.*
- *People are safer when they are in regulated services.*
- *People are safer when they have staff who are trained in a particular way.*
- *People are safer when their staff have had police checks (CRBs).*

COMMENT

There is no right or wrong answer to each statement but it might help you to consider what we mean by safety. Can an environment, inspection regime, training programme or strict monitoring guarantee safety? While all four aspects may at some level enhance safety for an individual, we need to be careful that we are not lulled into a false sense of achieving safety. If we take the example of institutional living, there is much literature documenting the devaluing experiences individuals have lived through (Grant et al., 2005). Similarly, research from Action on Elder Abuse *(2004) found that the risk of being abused was 9.9 times greater if you lived in a registered care home compared with living at home. While CRBs will tell us something about someone's criminal history, they cannot tell us everything about their past and will not inform us of any change to that situation. The reality is that we can never be assured of complete safety, and services have never been and probably never will be immune from abusive individuals and practices.*

In Chapter 2 we explored the notion of citizenship, which understands the person as being central to any process rather than a passive recipient of care. It focuses on how the individual engages with society at different levels both in terms of accessing support and also contributing to that community. It could be argued, therefore, that strengthening citizenship for individuals will keep them more connected with neighbours, friends and communities and will subsequently provide another layer of safety. If someone is known, connected and valued within their community, this may reduce their risk compared with being isolated and hidden away from the wider community (Duffy and Gillespie, 2009). While principles of choice, freedom and flexibility dominate much of the agenda and literature, Duffy and Gillespie suggest that careful consideration and planning have been taken in the implementation of this self-directed support. In particular, attention to risk assessment and risk management is central and can be mapped to each stage of the process. If we take the key stages of assessment, support planning and reviewing, we will see how this might work in practice.

Risk management

Assessment

The person will still be assessed under section 47 of the NHS and Community Care Act 1990. Right from the first contact, the assessment will be alert to any information that may signal potential abuse or high levels of risk. Within the assessment process both the service user and the professional will be required to highlight any risks as part of the process. At this point it may be necessary for the professional to act upon information or any concerns. At times the notion of self-assessment has been misinterpreted as meaning that the assessed needs will be based purely on the perception of the service user. In reality, self-assessment is a mechanism used to ensure service users are fully involved in the process. It does not mean that the professional takes a back seat and relies on the service user's assessment. Their role is to challenge and question and to provide alternative evidence if required. In this way any concerns about risk or potential risk can be identified and discussed at an early stage. Where a difference of opinion in relation to need or risk between the service user and social worker exists, there is a framework to deal with the discrepancies (see discussion on risk enablement panels below).

Support planning

At this stage of the process, there is a requirement for the service user to indicate how they intend to manage any risks either in relation to the support or managing the money. This encourages service users to think carefully and methodically about any potential risks that might occur. The role of the professional is to evaluate the plan and offer construc-tive advice. At times this may mean rejecting a plan based on the lack of attention or detail to risk management. In this way the service user is clear about the requirements and therefore motivated to complete this process diligently in order to get it signed off. Several local authorities have set up procedures to deal with risk management at this stage of the process.

Risk enablement panels are proving to be a successful mechanism. Some of the common features of risk enablement panels include:

- sharing risk decision-making where there are concerns about managing the level of risk;
- providing support, guidance and direction to staff, including conflict resolution;
- providing consistency;
- improving the management of risk decision-making including the focus on the risk to maintaining independence;
- sharing the responsibility for the management of complex risk cases;
- developing the learning and disseminating through existing communication methods.

(Putting People First, 2009)

Reviewing

The review process focuses on the outcomes identified in the support plan. In this sense the review process itself is personalised to fit the needs and the risks faced by the individual rather than being a standardised process. As the service users control the support plan, they also need to demonstrate how the outcomes have been met. One key aspect of the review will be to focus on the management of risk. Again the service user will be expected to demonstrate and sometimes evidence how they are managing risks. This may include financial risks but could extend to other risks to themselves or others. Duffy and Gillespie (2009, p. 10) believe that:

> *Shifting the primary focus of planning towards the individual and those closer to them, it increases the possibility of generating high quality plans and solutions but more importantly by shifting the role of the local authority to one of interrogator, checker and approver it encourages a creative dialogue that radically reduces the risk of ill considered plans and services.*

It is the role of the social worker to time the reviews to reflect relative risks and the possibility of significant changes of need. For some individuals a review may need to be scheduled after a month of the first payment, whereas for support plans where there is less likelihood of risk, the review may be more appropriately timed for six months.

ACTIVITY 6.5

Read the case study below and consider the questions in relation to risk assessment and risk management.

CASE STUDY

Tina is a 38-year-old single woman with progressive deteriorating multiple sclerosis. She is a permanent user of a wheelchair. She has a daughter, Helen, who is 20 years old. Helen is blind. Tina and Helen live together and Helen attends a local university. For the past year, Tina has been confined to sleeping downstairs in her terraced house, using a commode at night.

Continued

Tina has been allocated to a social worker for some years and has recently completed a self-assessment with a view to accessing an individual budget. She completed the assessment with the help of her daughter Helen. They both tried carefully to assess her needs and risks. Tina identified her need to sleep upstairs as she does not like being downstairs during the night as well as the day. She wants to be near her daughter at night so she can help her get to the toilet and back into bed. Tina has identified a decline in her mental well-being since she has been confined to sleeping downstairs. Ideally Tina would like a stair-lift to enable her to get upstairs at night. The social worker along with other health professionals agreed that there was a risk to Tina's mental well-being but were also concerned that a stair-lift would present other risks to both Tina and Helen. The occupational therapist (OT) was concerned that the occasional uncontrolled spasms Tina experiences would put her at risk if she were to use a stair-lift. The OT was also concerned that the equipment might pose a risk to Helen's safety on and around the stairs, both at the top and the bottom.

Because there were a number of points of disagreement between Tina's self-assessment and the professional assessment of the OT, the case was referred to the risk enablement panel to fully explore the situation. The panel was made up of a senior manager from the local authority, the social worker and the OT. Tina also attended part of the panel to present her own views. The panel carefully considered all aspects and were able to explore various risk-management tools which might provide a way forward. The panel eventually agreed that with careful planning, safeguards could be put in place and Tina and Helen should be allowed to choose to take the risks involved. The panel also insisted on a clear detailed support plan in relation to the risks identified before the individual budget could be agreed.

Tina knew she wanted to go ahead with the stair-lift and made some enquiries about which would be the most suitable type given her situation. Tina and Helen asked the social worker to support them in identifying the risks and exploring possible options. In this way Tina used the social worker to challenge her decisions and to act as a critical friend to ensure everything had been considered before the support plan was completed and ready for the risk enablement panel to see. Some of the detail referred to Tina and Helen having an agreed routine for each morning and night to ensure consistency and safety at all times and accepting support from the OT before they used it independently. The support plan was checked by the social worker and then presented to the risk enablement panel. The panel agreed that the money could be signed off, and Tina received her individual budget.

A review was set up two weeks after the stair-lift had been installed. The panel had recommended a short review period due to the nature of the risks. The panel was satisfied that Tina could manage the finances and other aspects of her individual budget, so the focus of the review was the management of risks in relation to the stair-lift. The OT was asked to attend the review to provide a current assessment of the way the risks were being managed. At the review Tina and Helen reported no problems with the stair-lift.

Continued

107

Tina could feel that her spirits had already lifted. The review meeting concluded that Tina and Helen were managing the risks well and the outcome of improved mental well-being was already being achieved. The next review meeting was set for 12 months.

ACTIVITY 6.5 *continued*

Having read the case study, consider the following questions.

- *Were there any differences between the needs and risks perceived by Tina and the professionals?*

- *How did the self-assessment process deal with these differences?*

- *How useful was the support planning process in managing the risks?*

- *How was the review process personalised to consider safeguarding issues for Tina and Helen?*

- *If the panel had refused to allow the instalment of the stair-lift, what do you think the risks might have been for Tina and Helen?*

- *Can you think of any factors that might have encouraged the panel to decide the stair-lift was unsafe?*

COMMENT

Clearly the perception of need and risk can differ between the service user and the professional and this is not necessarily a problem. The important factor is that both the service user and the professional have an opportunity to articulate and evidence their assessments. By shifting the lead of the process to the service user, the social worker can question decisions and encourage the service user to carefully consider all options and scenarios. This is very different from a professionally led process whereby the service user is forced into questioning and challenging the perceived expert. The premise of self-directed support is that the social worker assumes a facilitative role and encourages the service user to be guided by their own expertise. There may, however, be situations where the risks are too high. For example, if Tina had periods where she became confused or Helen was a heavy drinker, the decision may have been different. In any risk assessment the role of the social worker is to consider both the risks involved in agreeing to a set of actions and the risks involved in refusing a set of actions. As a social worker you need to be acutely attuned to both the potential benefits and dangers associated with any intervention.

CHAPTER SUMMARY

In all social work practice good practitioners are committed essentially to two equally important fundamental notions of promoting independence and protecting individuals from harm. Most of the time these two principles can work together in harmony and form part of an effective support plan or care package. At times, however, these two fundamental notions appear at opposite ends of the spectrum as

Continued

CHAPTER SUMMARY *continued*

they compete for dominance in a given situation. For social workers accountable to both service users and statutory agencies, the ability to carefully balance notions of care and control can be the most challenging aspect of social work. To deny someone their rights and wishes or to risk potential harm or loss of life is a dilemma that few professions have to consider on a daily basis.

It is perhaps no great surprise that the issue of safeguarding and personalisation is so contentious as practitioners, managers, policy-makers and academics grapple with these competing priorities. The way we connect with these two agendas may well influence how we position ourselves along this spectrum. It is also important to note that while research has indicated areas of concern, it has also reported a lack of knowledge about what is meant by personalisation. Suspicion and scepticism have risen as adult social work is changing under the current political/economic context. For some, there is a real sense that personalisation will be used to justify the rationalisation of social workers, leaving individuals vulnerable and unsupported. For those more optimistic of the compatibility of these two agendas, there is a sense that personalisation can lead to improving the safety of vulnerable people as risk management is personalised, and safeguarding becomes part of wider notions of citizenship.

The future of the social work role within a personalisation context continues to dominate much of the debate. A fear that vulnerable people will be left using unregulated services with no support is coupled with a concern whether social workers will actually be needed in the future. Alternatively, social work may have a great deal to offer in this new agenda. Advocates of personalisation recognise that some individuals can manage and support most aspects of their support including the management of risk, but many others will require professionally skilled individuals to guide them through this process. Some individuals may lack capacity to independently manage or organise their support. They may have very complex support needs, with a range of agencies involved. They may require the development of robust monitoring mechanisms to ensure they are safe and well. At such times the skilled professional can bring knowledge and expertise to guide and support people through this process. It is important, however, that the practitioner understands and embraces the principles of self-directed support in such instances. Self-directed support is about individuals having as much control as they can, to choose and guide the support and services they receive. It may, therefore, be possible to locate the skills social workers bring to this role with the people who will benefit most from it, rather than trying so hard to standardise the approach for individuals and therefore missing an opportunity to personalise support to individuals.

This chapter has identified and explored legislative, policy and other specific issues relating to personalisation and safeguarding. The chapter has also attempted to convey the genuine concern held by practitioners in pursuing these two agendas, while unravelling some of the misconceptions that have emerged. Finally, it is important to note that it is not uncommon for a change in policy direction to raise differences both ideologically and in relation to implementation, and that continued debate and research are a healthy and inevitable part of this evolving process.

FURTHER READING

Duffy, S and Gillespie, J (2009) *Personalisation and safeguarding*. London: In Control.

This useful paper provides a refreshing and somewhat challenging way of looking at personalisation and safeguarding.

Henwood, M and Hudson, B (2007) *Here to stay? Self-directed support: Aspiration and implementation (a review for the Department of Health).* Heathencote: Melanie Henwood Associates.

This accessible piece of research highlights the different perceptions of practitioners and managers in relation to self-directed support.

Manthorpe, J, Stevens, M, Rapaport, J, Harns, J, Jacobs, S, Challis, D, Netten, A, Knapp, M, Wilberforce, M and Glendinning, C (2009) Safeguarding and system change: Early perceptions of the implications for adult protection services of the English individual budget pilots. A qualitative study. *British Journal of Social Work*, 39: 1465–80.

It is important that you take time to study this first formal evaluation of individual budgets. It is an accessible report and highlights some of the early messages that have emerged.

WEBSITES

www.in-control.org.uk

www.communitycare.org.uk

Chapter 7
Preparing for practice:
The social work role

This chapter will enable you to become familiar with the following National Occupational Standards.

Key role 1: Prepare for, and work with individuals, families, carers, groups and communities to assess their needs and circumstances.

- Work with individuals, families and carers, groups and communities to enable them to assess and make informed decisions.
- Assess needs and options to recommend a course of action.

Key role 2: Plan, carry out, review and evaluate social work practice, with individuals, families, carers, groups, communities, and other professionals.

- Prepare, produce, implement and evaluate plans with individuals, families carers, groups, communities and professional colleagues.

Key role 3: Support individuals to represent their needs, views and circumstances.

- Advocate with, and on behalf of, individuals, families, carers, groups and communities.

Key role 6: Demonstrate professional competence in social work.

- Manage complex ethical issues, dilemmas and conflicts.

This chapter will also refer to the General Social Care Council Codes of Practice for social care workers (GSCC, 2002), which state the following.

As a social care worker you must protect the rights and promote the interests of service users and carers.

- Supporting service users' rights to control their lives and make informed choices about the services they receive (1.3).

As a social care worker you must strive to establish the trust and confidence of service users and carers.

- Communicate in an appropriate, open, accurate and straightforward way (2.2).

As a social care worker, you must respect the rights of service users while seeking to ensure that their behaviour does not harm themselves or other people.

- Recognising that service users have the right to take risks and helping them to identify and manage potential and actual risks to themselves and others (4.1).

This chapter will also introduce you to the following academic standards as set out in the 2008 social work subject benchmark statement.

5.5.1 Manage problem-solving activities.
5.5.2 Gathering information.
5.5.3 Analysis and synthesis.
5.5.4 Intervention and evaluation.
5.6 Communication skills.
5.7 Skills in working with others.

Introduction

In this chapter I will establish how you, as a student social worker practising within a personalisation context, can demonstrate competence in accordance with the National Occupational Standards and the GSCC Code of Practice (Topss England, 2002; GSCC, 2002). A great source of anxiety for students during practice placements often concerns the requirement that they demonstrate their abilities to relate theory to practice. Working within a personalisation context can really help with this, because the values, principles and theoretical perspectives underpinning the personalisation agenda are very much in accordance with social work values.

Table 7.1 illustrates the mapping exercise which was devised by Ali Gardner (MMU, 2009), in which she has identified specific ways that students should demonstrate competence in relation to the National Occupational Standards when working within a personalisation context.

Table 7.1

Key role	Personalisation context
1. Prepare for, and work with individuals, families, carers, groups and communities to assess their needs and circumstances.	• The emphasis on self assessment must be recognised by students. • A thorough understanding of a person-centred approach in all aspects of work must be employed and reflected upon in meeting this key role. • Students need to understand their role as *advisers* and *navigators* in making recommendations for appropriate courses of action. Students need to demonstrate how they have supported individuals and families to design and arrange appropriate support packages.
2. Plan, carry out, review and evaluate social work practice, with individuals, families, carers, groups, communities and other professionals.	Students must: • Consider how they support individuals to maintain as much choice and control over their own lives. • Demonstrate how they support individuals to plan and design their own packages of support. • Demonstrate their understanding and application of legal/policy directives and guidance in relation to personalisation. • Evidence their knowledge about processes, local resources and support. • Demonstrate how they support individuals to take a central role in co-ordinating and reviewing packages of support wherever appropriate. • Strive to evidence their role as an enabler and avoid taking on the role as the *expert*. They must therefore evidence how they have valued and respected individuals' decisions and chosen options. • Consider the benefits of group work when working with service users. Students should consider how family, friends and natural support networks can be supported to work positively with individuals. • Demonstrate their ability to identify and respond appropriately to any risk. Students must evidence decisions to intervene, demonstrating awareness of balancing risk and choice at all times. • Demonstrate how they support individuals to develop robust safeguarding measures for themselves.

Table 7.1 *continued*

3. Support individuals to represent their needs, views and circumstances.	Students must: • Demonstrate their awareness of the role of advocacy and identify when independent advocacy is required. • Evidence their ability to support individuals and families through self-assessment and support planning processes. • Evidence how individuals and their families have made decisions in written documents and reports. • Demonstrate good knowledge of local processes relating to resource allocation or other financial processes and an ability to share this knowledge in a transparent manner with individuals and their families.
4. Manage risk to individuals, families, carers, groups, communities, self and colleagues.	Students must: • Evidence their knowledge of national and local policies in relation to safeguarding and personalisation. • Demonstrate their ability to identify and respond appropriately to any risk. Students must evidence decisions to intervene, demonstrating awareness of balancing risk and choice at all times. • Demonstrate how they support individuals to develop robust safeguarding measures for themselves. • Demonstrate their ability to communicate concerns with individuals to support them in making safe choices about any support they access.
5. Manage and be accountable, with supervision and support, for your own social work practice within your organisation.	• Through supervision students should reflect on their social work role and consider issues of power, choice and control. Students should reflect on their ability to enable and support individuals to make their own decisions and design their own packages of support. • Students should demonstrate how they have used research and training to develop their understanding of personalisation and the role of the social worker.
6. Demonstrate professional competence in social work practice.	Students should: • Evidence how they have used supervision to develop their knowledge, skills and values in relation to personalisation. • Evidence how they have used supervision to manage complex ethical issues, dilemmas and conflicts in relation to supporting individuals to access personalised services. • Demonstrate how they have supported other team members or external colleagues to develop their understanding of the personalisation agenda.

Embedding personalisation. Manchester Metropolitan University, 2009

This table contains a lot of information, and rather than become overwhelmed by it, I suggest that you initially focus on Key role 1. You do not need to wait until you are on placement to begin considering how to apply the principles of personalisation to your practice. This can in fact become an important aspect of your preparation for practice. The activities in this chapter should help you to begin thinking about ways to apply these principles to your practice. Some of the activities, particularly Activities 7.5 and 7.6, present quite complex dilemmas, and it is highly likely that your practice educator would not expect you, as a student, to manage this level of complexity without additional support. The intention behind including these activities is to give you a sense of progressing through your social work course as you work through the chapter, with a view to considering practice dilemmas that you may subsequently encounter when practising as a qualified social worker.

ACTIVITY 7.1

- *Key role 1, Unit 2: Work with individuals, families, carers, groups and communities to help them make informed decisions*

- *Key role 1, Unit 3: Assess needs and options to recommend a course of action*

Taking Key role 1, Units 2 and 3, consider how you would carry out your work in a way that would maximise the service user's control over the assessment process, if you were going to work with the following service user.

- *A 60-year-old Asian man who has recently had a stroke, resulting in paralysis of his left arm and leg, and some difficulties with speech.*

COMMENT

You may have considered different ways to maximise the service user's communication – possibly using visual aids. You may have thought about ways to encourage the service user to think creatively about what he wants to happen, and what he would like to achieve, taking his culture and ethnicity into account.

ACTIVITY 7.2

Following on from this, now begin to write up an account of your practice in this case so far, as evidence of your competence. This needs to be much more than a description of what took place. Ideally it should include the rationale for your actions, a short critique of how you conducted your practice, and exploration of the values underpinning your practice.

COMMENT

As you work through the individual elements that constitute these two units, you will become aware that some of the terminology used does not reflect the empowering language used throughout the personalisation discourse. For example, Unit 3 requires that you: Assess needs and options to recommend a course of action. *While this does not directly refer to self-assessment, it also does not rule out self-assessment. Therefore it becomes your task to explain how you incorporated self-assessment into this process. As has already been established in Chapters 3 and 6, in practice self-assessment actually means assessment that is carried out jointly, with the service user taking the lead role. The National Occupational Standards for social work were drafted in broad, non-prescriptive terms, so that they could be applied flexibly to a range of different placement settings and allow for interpretation which is specific to the placement setting and service user group.*

Similarly, in relation to devising support packages, the above mapping exercise highlights that your role is that of adviser or navigator. This is a fundamentally different role to that of a care manager, the professional role that was introduced by the NHS and Community Care Act 1990 (DH, 1990). Social workers undertaking a care manager role are required to carry out assessments of service users' needs, in consultation with service users and carers, and then to proceed to organise care packages to meet those assessed needs. The care manager role has unfortunately become predominantly associated with gatekeeping functions. It is a much more directive role than that of an adviser or navigator, and one that puts the professional at the centre of the decision-making process. Self-directed support processes reverse the care management roles, by putting the service user at the centre, and therefore social workers are required to adapt to fulfil other, arguably more creative and fulfilling, roles (Leadbeater et al., 2008).

Encouragingly, Higham (2006) argues that social work practice has a distinct holistic quality, which enables social workers to practise in a range of situations, with a range of different people, and to be open to developing new roles. It is this *amorphous nature* that will enable social work to embrace and develop further new roles (Higham, 2006, p. 110). Higham goes on to suggest that social workers are ideally suited to undertaking the service navigator role, viewing this role as one in which the navigator *acts as an ongoing guide and pilot through the complexities of service provision* (Higham, 2006, p. 108). She stresses that the navigator role involves establishing a relationship with the service user, and that there is ongoing contact. Again, this contrasts with the care manager role, in which there is minimal contact after the care package is established, with this contact usually taking the form of a six-monthly or yearly review, which may not always be carried out by a qualified social worker.

If you now move to consider Key role 2 in the mapping exercise in Table 7.1, you can see that the emphasis is on *supporting people to design their own packages of support*. In Chapter 4, it became clear that while there continues to be uncertainty about a distinctive role for social workers within personalised services, feedback from service users regarding social work support was very positive. The evaluation conducted by In Control, for example, found that service users reported improvements in their quality of life, and their choice and control over their lives, if they had been supported by a social worker when they were planning their self-directed support (Hatton et al., 2008). Social workers may find it easier than other allied professionals to work in personalised ways because the philosophy and values of the social work profession are so closely aligned with the ethos of self-directed support (Tyson, 2009). Social workers have traditionally been advocates of service user self-determination, and in fact many social workers in the adult social care field had become disillusioned with their care management roles, which didn't align so closely with their value base. In their research for the Demos report *Making it personal*, Leadbeater and co-authors found that some professionals saw the implementation of self-directed support as a chance to *re-discover social work*. The majority of professionals who were consulted reported that their jobs had improved, now that they were working directly with service users to try to devise solutions, rather than functioning as gatekeepers or administrators (Leadbeater et al., 2008, p. 13).

The whole thrust of the personalisation agenda is that service users are provided with appropriate support which enables them to have more choice and control. Therefore personalisation does not require an abdication of professional support; rather it entails a reframing of this support. One very valuable way that social workers can help service users with support planning involves gaining and then sharing an extensive knowledge of the community resources available. The evaluation of In Control's third phase, from 2008 to 2009, indicates that many service users are developing support plans that include significant use of ordinary community facilities, with less dependence on traditional in-house social care services. This evaluation found that only 26 per cent of all respondents used some of their personal budgets to purchase traditional in-house social care services (Tyson et al., 2010). However, service users can only realistically make choices if they are fully aware of what alternatives actually exist, and are provided with reliable information about the quality of provision available. As Marian Barnes had identified in relation to direct payments, the notion of *empowerment by exit* – whereby dissatisfied service users can exit an unsatisfactory service if they are directly paying for it – can only work if service users have a better alternative to move to (Barnes, 1997, p. 34). Knowledge of provision and alternatives represents the *key to capability in a consumer society* (Higham, 2006, p. 108). The importance of providing this knowledge is highlighted in the present coalition government's *Vision for adult social care* (DH, 2010e), which stresses the need for up-to-date and accessible information about the range of services available, including information about the *quality of providers* (Office of Fair Trading/Frontier Economics, 2010, cited in DH, 2010e, p. 16).

ACTIVITY 7.3

Log on to the website for In Control at www.in-control.org.uk/ and follow the link under Information to the 'How to be in control DVD'. This is divided into the seven steps of self-directed support, and at each step you can download transcripts of discussions that took place with service users, carers, personal assistants and individual budget project leads. Alternatively, you can follow a link should you wish to purchase the DVD.

You may notice in Step 2 that service users and carers stress the importance of being able to produce non-traditional support plans. One of the individual budget project leads points out that some service users needed reassurance that it was acceptable to think imaginatively about ways to meet outcomes. Can you think of ways that you might encourage service users to devise their own unique support plans?

The In Control website is an extremely valuable source of information and I recommend that you allocate time to explore it thoroughly.

COMMENT

You may have considered introducing service users who are developing their support plans to individuals who are currently receiving self-directed support. You will hopefully have recognised the importance for you as a social work student to find out what services and facilities are available in the local community where you have been placed.

As you saw in Chapter 3, one of the stages in setting up an individual budget involves the service user getting agreement for the support plan. As Leadbeater points out, a support plan, rather than representing a 'wish list', must specify how it will meet the service user's needs and outcomes in acceptable ways (Leadbeater et al., 2008). Social workers' skills and experience may prove very useful at this stage. The findings from In Control's Total Transformation Project indicate that social workers have experience in challenging support plans, to ensure that they are fit for purpose (Tyson, 2009). They can also make effective use of relevant care management experience which will have included advocating on behalf of service users to secure funding.

It is useful at this stage to look at Key role 3 in the mapping exercise above, and with this in mind, consider the following scenarios.

ACTIVITY 7.4

Social worker 1

When Mr Saville was told that he was now eligible for an individual budget, his social worker told him not to worry about this, as it wouldn't make a big difference to his day-to-day experience of support services. She explained that he could leave it as a 'virtual' budget that she would use to pay for his support services. When Mr Saville asked how much money was in his virtual budget, she said she didn't want him to concern himself with all that, and reassured him that she would advocate for him, and make sure that there were no changes to his current support package.

Social worker 2

When Mrs Daly was told that she was now eligible for an individual budget, her social worker spent time with her, explaining what this meant, and how the self-assessment and support planning process would work. She then arranged extra visits to enable Mrs Daly to work through the whole process. She clarified how the local authority would work out the actual amount of money Mrs Daly would be entitled to. She encouraged Mrs Daly to think creatively about how she wanted to have her needs met, providing information about a whole range of facilities in her local community. However, she also explained that the resulting support plan would have to clearly meet Mrs Daly's needs and outcomes. She helped Mrs Daly to consider combining different options, to stay within the budget.

• *Referring to the mapping exercise in Table 7.1 as a guide, try to identify where there is evidence for Key role 3 within each of these scenarios.*

COMMENT

You may have identified that social worker 2 is practising within a personalisation context, and she provides a range of evidence to demonstrate her practice competence. There is also evidence of her adherence to the Code of Practice, which we will consider shortly.

In the last chapter, you considered issues relating to the safeguarding of adults, and one of the case studies illustrated a way of working with the service user Jude, to reduce risks related to her employing unsuitable personal assistants. This empowering approach to your practice is crucial if you are going to practise within a personalisation context.

In order to demonstrate competence in relation to Key role 4, you will need to provide evidence of the ways you have assessed and managed any potential risks to service users, to yourself or to colleagues. There is a fine balance to be struck between managing risk and promoting choice, and each situation will have to be considered carefully. Keeping in mind that your role is that of a facilitator, your aim is to encourage service users to consider and explore any potential risks inherent in their support planning. This is a very different risk-management approach to the more traditional 'expert' approach, in which the professional determines what constitutes risk, and also what can be considered acceptable risk. Within this personalised approach, you are aiming at facilitating a dialogue about any potential risks, and also any possible ways to minimise risks.

This theme of risk management as opposed to risk elimination is acknowledged in the government's *Vision for adult social care* (DH, 2010e), to ensure that service users have maximum choice and control over their support and are recognised as the *experts in their own lives* (DH, 2010e, p. 26).

Key roles 5 and 6 require you to focus on your own professional development and social work practice. Since this relates to your understanding of the social work role, it can present quite a challenge, because of the changing nature of the social work role. The social work role in adult services has had to adapt to major policy changes over recent decades, with marketisation dominating from the mid-1980s through the 1990s, followed by a move towards increasing modernisation and managerialism from 1997 onwards. Jones and co-authors argue that this has resulted in contemporary social workers *often doing little more than supervising the deterioration of people's lives* (Jones et al., 2010b, p. 1). This echoes a view put forward by Davies (1994) that social work has a maintenance function, since social work practice helps to maintain the stability of society. Similarly, Thompson (2009) has put forward the suggestion that social workers can be faced with the task of *patching up* a failed welfare system, and therefore can sometimes feel they are *doing society's dirty work* (Thompson, 2009, p. 7).

As you work through the many ways you can demonstrate your competence by practising within a personalisation context, hopefully you will recognise that by working in this empowering way, social workers are helping to ensure that service users can achieve a good quality of life, with maximum choice and control. In this way, assisting with the implementation of self-directed support really can provide an opportunity to rediscover social work as an ethical and anti-oppressive career choice, with the potential to bring about positive change in people's lives (Jones et al., 2010b).

Evidence for the Codes of Practice

I have begun this chapter with a consideration of ways that you can provide evidence of your competence in relation to the National Occupational Standards, and this evidence will contain direct references to the values underpinning your practice. However, it is crucial that you also provide evidence which demonstrates your understanding of the centrality of the values underpinning social work. As Parker argues, since social workers engage with vulnerable people, making decisions that impact on their lives, they must work in accordance with *transparent understandable principles* (Parker, 2010, p. 2). The values underpinning social work practice are not unique to social work – many are shared with allied professions. However, the commitment to anti-oppressive and anti-discriminatory practice, which includes a commitment to actively challenge discrimination and oppression, may indeed be unique to the social work profession. It is not considered sufficient to *identify and analyse discrimination, racism, disadvantage, inequality and injustice. Social workers are required to take action to counter that discrimination* (Shardlow and Nelson, 2005, p. v).

The value requirements for social work practice are contained within the GSCC Code of Practice (GSCC, 2002).

Table 7.2 represents another part of the mapping exercise developed by Ali Gardner, as part of the Embedding Personalisation conference (MMU, 2009). The table focuses on specific ways in which students should address the Codes of Practice, when working within a personalisation context.

Table 7.2 *Record of evidence for Code Of Practice*

Code of Practice	Evidence – Personalisation context
Safeguard and promote the interests of service users and carers.	Students must: • Demonstrate how they have supported individuals to identify needs and choices and considered both opportunities and potential risks involved. • Evidence how they have informed individuals and their families in relation to developing personalised packages of support. • Evidence how they have supported individuals and their families to resolve any conflict or difference of opinion in designing and achieving personalised support. • Support families and carers to identify the level of support they can provide in caring for individuals in a way which respects family loyalties and maintains their own well-being.
Strive to maintain the trust and confidence of service users and carers.	Students must: • Evidence how they have worked with individuals in a way which is transparent, honest and realistic in relation to assessment and funding resources. • Demonstrate how they have shared information regarding the financial processes attached to the personalisation of support with individuals and their families. • Evidence how they have worked with individuals and their families within a person-centred framework. • Demonstrate how they have supported individuals and families to lead the assessment of need and designing of support.
Promote the independence of service users and protect them as far as possible from danger or harm.	Students must: • Evidence how they have worked with individuals to enable them to make informed decisions and balance opportunities and risks within designing their own support. • Demonstrate how they have supported both individuals and their families where there may be a difference of opinion in relation to perceived risks and opportunities. • Evidence their ability to provide a professional opinion in relation to potential danger or harm where they have not been identified by individuals and families. • Demonstrate how they have managed these differences in opinion while ensuring the individual remains in control of their own support. *Continued*

Code of Practice	Evidence – Personalisation context
Table 7.2 *Continued*	
Respect the rights of service users while seeking to ensure their behaviour does not harm themselves or other people.	Students must: • Demonstrate how they have worked with individuals to support them to achieve outcomes. • Demonstrate how they have worked within a person-centred framework which respects individual choice. • Demonstrate how they have supported individuals and their families to have the confidence and skills to assess their own needs. • Evidence how they have negotiated area of tension between professional and personal opinion and any conflicts or tensions within family or caring networks. • Evidence their ability to be honest and transparent with all aspects of the assessment from the beginning of the process. • Demonstrate an ability to identify any behaviours or decisions which could lead to potential harm of other people. • Demonstrate how they have managed these situations while ensuring the individual remains in control of designing and achieving personalised support. • Demonstrate that they have reflected on some of these dilemmas within supervision.
Uphold public trust and confidence in social care services.	Students must: • Demonstrate their ability to work in a professional manner at all times. • Evidence their knowledge and ability to share knowledge in relation to personalised packages of support with individuals and their families at the outset of any assessment. • Demonstrate that they have explored all options in relation to the various ways for individuals and their families to achieve personalised support. • Demonstrate that they have worked in a transparent way and shared all relevant information regarding assessment, resource allocation and other information with individuals and their families where appropriate.
Be accountable for the quality of their work and take responsibility for maintaining and improving their knowledge and skills.	Students must: • Demonstrate current knowledge of legislation, policy and local procedures in relation to the personalisation agenda. • Demonstrate how they have shared this with individuals and their families at the beginning of any input. • Evidence how they have used supervision and peer support to develop their knowledge and skills in relation to enabling individuals to achieve personalised packages of support. • Evidence how they have supported other team members or external colleagues in developing knowledge, skills and awareness in relation to personalisation.

Embedding Personalisation. Manchester Metropolitan University, 2009

Again, there is a lot of information contained in this table for you to process, and you will need to spend some time going through each of the individual codes.

As you work through this table, you should start to see that working within a personalisation context can help you to devise strategies to address some of the dilemmas inherent in practising in accordance with the codes of practice. For example, promoting service users' independence and respecting their rights can be in tension with protecting service users and others from harm. When you examine the ways in which the author has proposed that students can provide evidence for the individual codes, it should become clear that working within a personalisation framework allows you to clearly articulate the values underpinning your practice.

ACTIVITY 7.5

Case study

Matthew is a 32-year-old man who has a diagnosis of schizophrenia. He also has a moderate learning disability. He has lived in supported accommodation for a number of years, but there have been concerns raised by the other tenants in this group home because Matthew has been setting small fires in his bedroom. The support workers have spoken to him about this, but other tenants say they can still smell burning in his room, and they want him to move out. Matthew would like to move into his own flat, but his parents think he needs considerably more support. They believe he should move into residential care as he needs more support than is provided at the group home. The support workers report that Matthew has some good independent living skills, but feel he needs prompting to eat regularly and to take his medication.

The Code of Practice requires you to:

> Respect the rights of service users while seeking to ensure their behaviour does not harm themselves or others.

With reference to the mapping exercise in Table 7.2, go through each of the eight points raised in relation to this element of the Code of Practice, and consider how you would relate these to your work with Matthew.

COMMENT

Social workers are frequently faced with the challenge of balancing the rights and welfare of the individual with the sometimes competing needs of the wider community. When addressing this dilemma, social workers can find themselves in the unenviable position of having to exercise care and control simultaneously, as they endeavour to respect the individual's right to take risks, while also striving to keep people safe (Thompson, 2009).

You may have found that working through the points in Table 7.2 helped you to navigate your way through this dilemma.

Using the same case study, you can work through the other codes, to see if the points highlighted there are equally useful.

Barnard (2008, p. 15) has described the current phase of social work as the *risk management period*, with the implication that because of professional liability, the tendency is to emphasise safety, at the expense of an individual's right to take risks. You have seen in the last exercise that working within a personalisation context can help to address the dilemma for social workers who have responsibilities towards individuals and also the wider community. Parker (2010) introduces the concept that service user self-determination can be understood as a positive freedom or a negative freedom. The negative freedom suggests that people should be able to make choices, to accept or refuse services *without interference from others* even if they are *at risk of self harm*. Conversely, positive freedom suggests that while people should be able to make choices *wherever possible ... there are limitations and some people will need protection from harm by self or others* (Parker, 2010, p. 7).

ACTIVITY **7.6**

With this concept as a guide, consider the following case study.

Alan is a 22-year-old man who has a progressive visual impairment. His sight has deteriorated rapidly over the last six months, and he now has only partial sight in one eye. His hobby for many years has been motorbike mechanics, and he spends a lot of time working on an old motorbike that belonged to his father. He lives a short distance from your office – about two minutes by car. One day he arrives at your office, motorbike helmet in hand, and informs you that he has fixed the bike and has driven it here to show you.

Working within a personalisation context, how would you address the dilemma of care versus control inherent in this situation?

The Code of Practice requires you to:

> Promote the independence of service users while protecting them as far as possible from danger or harm.

Does the concept of a positive freedom help you to find a way through this dilemma?

Refer back to the mapping exercise in Table 7.2, and see if any of the points for this code are of assistance.

COMMENT

You may have considered the need to discuss with Alan the risks he potentially poses to himself and others, by driving a motorbike when his vision is so restricted. However, you will probably have explored ways to impart this information, so that Alan is very much taking part in a dialogue about risk management and risk minimisation.

Practice educators

Practice educators are given the task of identifying learning opportunities in their workplaces that will enable social work students to achieve and demonstrate competence in practice. Part of this process involves considering the composite units and elements of the National Occupational Standards and the Codes of Practice in order to devise learning plans that will help students to apply the individual/required standards to the distinctive agency they are placed in. For practice educators who are encouraging their students to practise in accordance with the principles of personalisation and self-directed support, the mapping exercises included in this chapter may prove a useful tool to help with formulating an appropriate practice curriculum (Parker, 2010, p. 66). Tables 7.1 and

7.2 may also help to stimulate debate and exploration within supervision regarding the complexities of implementing self-directed support.

CHAPTER SUMMARY

This chapter has focused on ways in which social work students can begin to relate personalisation to their practice, in order to consolidate their understanding of the personalisation agenda and identify further learning needs. Some quite complex practice dilemmas have been presented, which will have encouraged students to consider how to apply the principles of personalisation and self-directed support in complicated situations.

It is anticipated that this chapter will also have contained some useful material for qualified social work practitioners working within a personalisation context. The National Occupational Standards and the Code of Practice continue to have a pivotal role for qualified social workers, guiding and informing their practice. Social work has a well-established tradition of reflective practice, and many of the dilemmas inherent in practising in accordance with these standards and codes necessitate in-depth consideration and reflection. Hopefully the points identified in Tables 7.1 and 7.2 will assist this reflective process.

FURTHER READING

Lomax, R, Jones, K, Leigh, S and Gay, C (2010) *Surviving your social work placement.* London: Palgrave Macmillan.

This book is a useful and informative guide for students undertaking practice placements. While it doesn't refer specifically to practice learning within a personalisation context, it contains a wealth of accessible information relating to the experience of learning on placement.

Parker, J (2010) *Effective practice learning in social work* (2nd edn). Exeter: Learning Matters.

This book covers all aspects of practice learning, and features a chapter on the social work value base, which links well with issues raised in this chapter. This book addresses many of the anxieties that students report, in relation to practice learning, and is therefore essential reading.

WEBSITES

www.in-control.org.uk

This website contains a wealth of information relating to policy, practice and experience from people directing their own support.

www.scie.org.uk

This website will keep you informed of up-to-date developments related to personalisation. It currently contains a range of resources to help implement the government's *Vision for adult social care* (DH, 2010e).

Conclusion

At the time of writing this book, personalisation as a concept was beginning to shape government thinking and practice in a variety of ways. At a local level, pilot sites had begun to report positive accounts and experiences of using self-directed support models. Service user narrative through research was emerging to report both the positive and negative aspects of this new way of working and the coalition government formed in 2010 was seeking to identify whether and how the model could be adapted to fit with their own emerging agenda and policy objectives. Early signals of its compatibility with 'Big Society' thinking were expressed with specific targets set within the Comprehensive Spending Review (2010) to extend the use of personal budgets across the full range of health and social care needs and also for children's services and special educational needs.

The political context of personalisation has been developed as a common thread throughout the book, recognising and analysing the way in which concepts of welfare have emerged and developed. The text has highlighted the significance of service user voice and its powerful influence in the development of self-directed support.

It is hoped that the reader has begun to understand the legislative, policy and practice models that have been developed for different service user groups and their carers in relation to self-directed support. The book has explored the subtle, yet significant, differences between care management and self-directed support using service user narrative to demonstrate some of the key themes and outcomes of this way of working. In addition, the inclusion of narrative has challenged the reader to consider broader issues of discrimination and empowerment which underpin one's understanding of personalisation.

Principally, personalisation is based on the person controlling and directing the support in a way that they believe will meet their needs. The book has considered how one of the key tensions surrounding choice and risk can be addressed within this framework. Drawing on research, practice experience and student activities, the book has attempted to provide a balanced picture of these contentious issues. Mindful of the polarisation of this debate, the book has considered some of the possible consequences for the social work role in the future.

While the book encourages students to adopt an evidence-based approach to their practice, it also recognises that many questions and uncertainties remain in relation to the implementation of personalisation. The future of adult social care is set to change dramatically and there are huge question marks in relation to the shape and function of the social work role. Qualifying students need to recognise the challenging contexts within which they will work. They also need to consider how they will adopt a questioning approach towards the way structures, organisations and practitioners adapt and respond to changing agendas, tasks and roles.

Fundamentally, the book has attempted to reinforce the need to bring together social work values and emerging practice by encouraging the reader to develop a radical engagement with key concepts and practical, effective solutions. In this way it provides an opportunity to embrace personalisation as more than a repackaged way of working but rather as a new paradigm of good practice.

Appendix

Subject benchmark for social work

Defining principles

4.6 Social work is a moral activity that requires practitioners to recognise the dignity of the individual, but also to make and implement difficult decisions (including restriction of liberty) in human situations that involve the potential for benefit or harm. Honours degree programmes in social work therefore involve the study, application of, and critical reflection upon, ethical principles and dilemmas. As reflected by the four care councils' codes of practice, this involves showing respect for persons, honouring the diverse and distinctive organisations and communities that make up contemporary society, promoting social justice and combating processes that lead to discrimination, marginalisation and social exclusion. This means that honours undergraduates must learn to:

- recognise and work with the powerful links between intrapersonal and interpersonal factors and the wider social, legal, economic, political and cultural context of people's lives;

- understand the impact of injustice, social inequalities and oppressive social relations;

- challenge constructively individual, institutional and structural discrimination;

- practise in ways that maximise safety and effectiveness in situations of uncertainty and incomplete information;

- help people to gain, regain or maintain control of their own affairs, insofar as this is compatible with their own or others' safety, well-being and rights;

- work in partnership with service users and carers and other professionals to foster dignity, choice and independence, and effect change.

4.7 The expectation that social workers will be able to act effectively in such complex circumstances requires that honours degree programmes in social work should be designed to help students learn to become accountable, reflective, critical and evaluative. This involves learning to:

- work in a transparent and responsible way, balancing autonomy with complex, multiple and sometimes contradictory accountabilities (for example, to different service users, employing agencies, professional bodies and the wider society);

- acquire and apply the habits of critical reflection, self-evaluation and consultation, and make appropriate use of research in decision-making about practice and in the evaluation of outcomes.

Subject knowledge, understanding and skills

Subject knowledge and understanding

5.1 During their degree studies in social work, graduates are expected to acquire, critically evaluate, apply and integrate knowledge and understanding in the following five core areas of study.

5.1.1 Social work services, service users and carers, which include:
- the social processes (associated with, for example, poverty, migration, unemployment, poor health, disablement, lack of education and other sources of disadvantage) that lead to marginalisation, isolation and exclusion, and their impact on the demand for social work services.

5.1.2 The service delivery context, which include:
- the location of contemporary social work within historical, comparative and global perspectives, including European and international contexts;

- the changing demography and cultures of communities in which social workers will be practising;

- the complex relationships between public, social and political philosophies, policies and priorities and the organisation and practice of social work, including the contested nature of these;

- the issues and trends in modern public and social policy and their relationship to contemporary practice and service delivery in social work;

- the significance of legislative and legal frameworks and service delivery standards (including the nature of legal authority, the application of legislation in practice, statutory accountability and tensions between statute, policy and practice);

- the current range and appropriateness of statutory, voluntary and private agencies providing community-based, day-care, residential and other services and the organisational systems inherent within these;

- the significance of interrelationships with other related services, including housing, health, income maintenance and criminal justice (where not an integral social service);

- the contribution of different approaches to management, leadership and quality in public and independent human services;

- the development of personalised services, individual budgets and direct payments;

- the implications of modern information and communications technology (ICT) for both the provision and receipt of services.

5.1.3 Values and ethics, which include:

- the nature, historical evolution and application of social work values;

- the moral concepts of rights, responsibility, freedom, authority and power inherent in the practice of social workers as moral and statutory agents;

- the complex relationships between justice, care and control in social welfare and the practical and ethical implications of these, including roles as statutory agents and in upholding the law in respect of discrimination;

- aspects of philosophical ethics relevant to the understanding and resolution of value dilemmas and conflicts in both interpersonal and professional contexts;

- the conceptual links between codes defining ethical practice, the regulation of professional conduct and the management of potential conflicts generated by the codes held by different professional groups.

5.1.4 Social work theory

5.1.5 The nature of social work practice

Subject-specific skills and other skills

Problem-solving skills

5.5 These are sub-divided into four areas:

5.5.1 Managing problem-solving activities: honours graduates in social work should be able to plan problem-solving activities, i.e. to:

- think logically, systematically, critically and reflectively;

- apply ethical principles and practices critically in planning problem-solving activities;

- plan a sequence of actions to achieve specified objectives, making use of research, theory and other forms of evidence;

- manage processes of change, drawing on research, theory and other forms of evidence.

5.5.2 Gathering information: honours graduates in social work should be able to:

- gather information from a wide range of sources and by a variety of methods, for a range of purposes. These methods should include electronic searches, reviews of relevant literature, policy and procedures, face-to-face interviews, written and telephone contact with individuals and groups;

- take into account differences of viewpoint in gathering information and critically assess the reliability and relevance of the information gathered;

- assimilate and disseminate relevant information in reports and case records.

5.5.3 Analysis and synthesis: honours graduates in social work should be able to analyse and synthesise knowledge gathered for problem-solving purposes, i.e. to:

- assess human situations, taking into account a variety of factors (including the views of participants, theoretical concepts, research evidence, legislation and organisational policies and procedures);

- analyse information gathered, weighing competing evidence and modifying their viewpoint in light of new information, then relate this information to a particular task, situation or problem;

- consider specific factors relevant to social work practice (such as risk, rights, cultural differences and linguistic sensitivities, responsibilities to protect vulnerable individuals and legal obligations);

- assess the merits of contrasting theories, explanations, research, policies and procedures;

- synthesise knowledge and sustain reasoned argument;

- employ a critical understanding of human agency at the macro (societal), mezzo (organisational and community) and micro (inter and intrapersonal) levels;

- critically analyse and take account of the impact of inequality and discrimination in work with people in particular contexts and problem situations.

5.5.4 Intervention and evaluation: honours graduates in social work should be able to use their knowledge of a range of interventions and evaluation processes selectively to:

- build and sustain purposeful relationships with people and organisations in community-based, and interprofessional contexts;

- make decisions, set goals and construct specific plans to achieve these, taking into account relevant factors including ethical guidelines;

- negotiate goals and plans with others, analysing and addressing in a creative manner human, organisational and structural impediments to change;

- implement plans through a variety of systematic processes that include working in partnership;

- undertake practice in a manner that promotes the well-being and protects the safety of all parties;

- engage effectively in conflict resolution;

- support service users to take decisions and access services, with the social worker as navigator, advocate and supporter;

- manage the complex dynamics of dependency and, in some settings, provide direct care and personal support in everyday living situations;

- meet deadlines and comply with external definitions of a task;

- plan, implement and critically review processes and outcomes;

- bring work to an effective conclusion, taking into account the implications for all involved;

- monitor situations, review processes and evaluate outcomes;

- use and evaluate methods of intervention critically and reflectively.

Communication skills

5.6 Honours graduates in social work should be able to communicate clearly, accurately and precisely (in an appropriate medium) with individuals and groups in a range of formal and informal situations, i.e. to:

- make effective contact with individuals and organisations for a range of objectives, by verbal, paper-based and electronic means;

- clarify and negotiate the purpose of such contacts and the boundaries of their involvement;

- listen actively to others, engage appropriately with the life experiences of service users, understand accurately their viewpoint and overcome personal prejudices to respond appropriately to a range of complex personal and interpersonal situations;

- use both verbal and non-verbal cues to guide interpretation;

- identify and use opportunities for purposeful and supportive communication with service users within their everyday living situations;

- follow and develop an argument and evaluate the viewpoints of, and evidence presented by others;

- write accurately and clearly in styles adapted to the audience, purpose and context of the communication;

- use advocacy skills to promote others' rights, interests and needs;

- present conclusions verbally and on paper, in a structured form, appropriate to the audience for which these have been prepared;

- make effective preparation for, and lead meetings in a productive way;

- communicate effectively across potential barriers resulting from differences (for example, in culture, language and age).

Skills in working with others

5.7 Honours graduates in social work should be able to work effectively with others, i.e. to:

- involve users of social work services in ways that increase their resources, capacity and power to influence factors affecting their lives;

- consult actively with others, including service users and carers, who hold relevant information or expertise;

- act cooperatively with others, liaising and negotiating across differences such as organisational and professional boundaries and differences of identity or language;

- develop effective helping relationships and partnerships with other individuals, groups and organisations that facilitate change;

- act with others to increase social justice by identifying and responding to prejudice, institutional discrimination and structural inequality;

- act within a framework of multiple accountability (for example, to agencies, the public, service users, carers and others);

- challenge others when necessary, in ways that are most likely to produce positive outcomes.

Glossary

Co-production This is a term used to describe a process whereby service users and the wider community are involved in designing services, support and solutions. The premise of co-production is that those using services are best placed to advise and design support. This process requires power being shared with service users to empower them to identify solutions. Co-production spans both local services/support to building social capital.

Direct payment This is a cash payment given to service users in lieu of services. The important issue in relation to personalisation is that direct payments legislation has made it permissible for local authorities to give service users money. Basically it is the mechanism required for transferring the money from the local authority to the service user.

Independent living movement This represents a worldwide movement of disabled people who proclaim to work for self-determinism, self-respect and equal opportunities. The movement emerged in the early 1970s with the development of Independent Centres for Independence. Advocates promote a way of looking at disability and society which promotes the social model of disability and believes that preconceived notions and a predominantly medical view of disability contribute to negative attitudes towards disabled people.

Independent living This is one of the goals of personalisation. It does not necessarily mean living on your own or doing things alone but focuses on people having a choice and control over the assistance and or equipment needed to go about their daily life.

Indicative budget/indicative allocation Once an assessment is complete, the local authority will use the resource allocation system to identify the level of financial support required. The service user is then informed of this amount of money. This knowledge helps the service user develop a support plan. Once the support plan has been agreed, the indicative budget will then become an actual budget and is given to the service user. It is called an indicative budget as the money cannot be transferred to the individual until the local authority is satisfied that the support plan will meet the needs identified in the assessment.

Individual budget Individual budgets include the money from the local authority as described under **Personal budget**, but it also involves bringing together different funding streams besides social care. This might include all or some of the following: local authority adult social care; integrated community equipment services; Disabled Facilities Grants; Supporting People for housing-related support; Access to Work and Independent Living Fund. This money is pooled to allow the service user flexibility in meeting their needs. Service users may choose to receive it as cash or services or a mixture of both.

The terms 'personal budget' and 'individual budget' are starting to be used interchangeably by some local authorities. This has caused confusion for service users and social workers alike but the notions of choice, control and flexibility underpin both definitions.

Outcome-focused review The support plan will identify a number of outcomes that the service user wants to achieve and how support will be arranged to achieve these. The purpose of an outcome-focused review is to review progress in using the budget to achieve the outcomes set out in the support plan. During the review the support plan may also be updated and the council will check if the person is still eligible for social care.

Personal budget This is the allocation of funding given to service users after an assessment. The service user can choose to take this money as a direct payment or can leave it with the local authority to commission the service or support. Either way it is important that the service user can choose how the money is spent. Importantly, service users know how much money has been allocated. See also **Individual budget**.

Personalisation This is the umbrella term used to encapsulate the government's agenda for the transformation of adult social care. The government use this term broadly to refer to individuals having as much choice and control in the way support is designed and delivered as possible and ensuring that universal and community support and services are available and accessible to everyone.

Person-centred planning This focuses on supporting individuals to live as independently as possible, having choice and control wherever possible. Person-centred planning places the individual at the centre of the process and builds support, networks and services around them.

Resource allocation system (RAS) This is a system used by most local authorities to work out the financial resources which will be allocated to the individual and takes place after the assessment.

Self-assessment Service users are given the opportunity to assess their own needs. This usually involves completing a self-assessment questionnaire whereby the service user scores their needs against a set of domains.

Self-directed support This idea forms the basis of personalisation. Service users are seen as the experts in their own lives. They are best placed to know what is best for them. No matter how service users choose to receive social care, the notion of self-determination should be fully embraced.

Support brokerage This is a term used to describe a range of tasks and functions carried out by an individual or organisation to support a service user to design, arrange and manage their support.

Support planning This is the process whereby service users can identify how they would like to live their life and choose the support or services that will help them make the changes. The support plan must identify how the budget will be spent, how it will meet the outcomes and how the person will stay in control of the plan.

Trust A trust can be a group of people made up of family and friends, chosen by the person receiving the budget. Individuals can also choose to employ a private or voluntary organisation that can look after the individual's budget on their behalf. An individual will usually have to make a payment to the organisation for this support.

References

Action on Elder Abuse (2004) *Hidden voices: Older people's experience of abuse. An analysis of calls to the action on elder abuse helpline.* London: Help the Aged.

Adams, R (2010) *The short guide to social work.* Bristol: Policy Press.

Adams, R, Dominelli, L and Payne, M (2009) *Critical practice in social work.* Exeter: Palgrave Macmillan.

ADASS (2008) *Personalisation and safeguarding prepared for ADASS executive council 21 October.* London: ADASS.

ADASS (2009) *Common resource allocation framework.* London: ADASS.

Ahmed, M (2008) *Social workers vague on personal budgets.* **www.communitycare.co.uk**

Armstrong, D (2003) *Experiences of special education.* London: Routledge/Falmer.

Atkinson, D (2005) Narratives and people with learning disabilities, in Grant, G, Goward, P, Richardson, M and Ramcharan, P (eds) *Learning disability. A life cycle approach to valuing people.* Berkshire: Open University Press.

Atkinson, R (1998) *The life story interview. Qualitative research methods.* London: Sage.

Barnard, A (2008) Values, ethics and professionalisation: A social work history, in Barnard, A, Horner, N and Wild, J (eds) *Value base of social work and social care: An active learning handbook.* Glasgow: Open University.

Barnes, C and Mercer, G (2010) *Exploring disability* (2nd edn). Cambridge: Policy Press.

Barnes, M (1997) *Care, communities and citizens.* London: Longman.

BASW (2002) *Code of ethics for social workers.* Birmingham: BASW.

Beresford, P (2003) *It's our lives: A short theory of knowledge, distance and experience.* London: Citizen Press.

Blyth, C and Gardner, A (2007) We're not asking for anything special: Direct payments and the carers of disabled children. *Disability and Society,* 22 (3): 235–49.

Borsay, A (2005) *Disability and social policy in Britain since 1750: A history of exclusion.* Basingstoke: Palgrave Macmillan.

Boyle, D, Clark, S and Burns, S (2006) *Co-production by people outside paid employment.* York: Joseph Rowntree Foundation.

Braye, S and Preston-Shoot, M (2001) *Empowering practice in social care.* Buckingham: Open University Press.

Braye, S and Preston-Shoot, M (2010) *Practising social work law* (3rd edn). Basingstoke: Palgrave Macmillan.

Brown, H and Benson, S (1992) *A practical guide to working with people with learning disabilities: A handbook for care assistants and support workers.* London: Hawker Publications.

Buck, T and Smith, S (2003) *Poor relief or poor deal: The social fund, safety nets and social security.* Hampshire: Ashgate Publishing Ltd.

Carlin, J and Lenehan, C (2006) Overcoming barriers to the take-up of direct payments by parents of disabled children, in Leece, J and Bornat, J (eds) *Developments in direct payments.* Bristol: Policy Press.

Carr, S and Robbins, D (2009) *The implementation of individual budget schemes in adult social care. Research Briefing 20.* London: Social Care Institute for Excellence.

Chinn, C (1995) *Poverty amidst prosperity: The urban poor in England, 1834–1914.* Manchester: Manchester University Press.

Clarke, J (2004) *Changing welfare, changing states: New directions in social policy.* London: Sage.

Community Care (2008) *Professional split over the future of adult social care. Social workers harbour doubts on personalization.* **www.communitycare.co.uk**

Coppock, V and Dunn, B (2010) *Understanding social work practice in mental health.* London: Sage.

Crosby, N (2008) Children and families in control. Self directed futures for children, young people and carers, in Hatton, C et al., *A report on In Control's second phase: Evaluation and learning 2005-2007.* London: In Control.

CSCI (2008a) *Cutting the cake fairly: CSCI review of eligibility criteria for social care.* Newcastle: CSCI.

CSCI (2008b) *Putting people first – equality and diversity matters 2: Providing appropriate services for black and minority ethnic people.* London: CSCI.

CSCI (2008c) *Putting people first – equality and diversity matters 1: Providing appropriate services for lesbian, gay and bisexual and transgender people.* London: CSCI.

CSCI (2009) *The state of social care in England 2007–2008.* London: CSCI.

Davies, M (1994) *The essential social worker: An introduction to professional practice in the 1990s* (3rd edn). Aldershot: Arena.

Davies, K (1998) The disabled people's movement – putting the power in empowerment. *Paper for a seminar at Sheffield University.* Sheffield: Sheffield University.

Department of Health (1989) *Caring for people: Community care in the next decade and beyond.* London: HMSO.

Department of Health (1990) *The NHS and Community Care Act.* London: HMSO.

Department of Health (1991) *Care management and assessment: Summary of practice guidance.* London: Department of Health.

Department of Health (1998) *Modernising social services: Promoting independence, improving protection, raising standards.* London: Department of Health.

Department of Health (2000) *No secrets: Guidance on developing and implementing multi-agency policies and procedures to procedures to protect vulnerable adults from abuse.* London: Department of Health.

Department of Health (2001) *Valuing people: A new strategy for learning disability for the 21st century.* London: Department of Health.

Department of Health (2003a) *Direct payments guidance: Community care, services for carers' and children's services (direct payments guidance).* London: Department of Health.

Department of Health (2003b) *Social services performance assessment framework indicators 2002–2003.* London: Department of Health.

Department of Health (2003c) *Fair access to care services – Guidance on eligibility for adult social care.* London: Department of Health.

Department of Health (2006) *Our health, our care, our say: A new direction for community service.* London: Department of Health.

Department of Health (2007a) *Putting people first: A shared vision and commitment to the transformation of adult social care.* London: Department of Health.

Department of Health (2007b) *Independence, choice and risk: A guide to best practice in supported decision making. Annex A. A supported decision tool.* London: Department of Health.

Department of Health (2008a) *Transforming social care.* LAC (DH) (2008). London: Department of Health.

Department of Health (2008b) *Putting people first – Working to make it happen:* Adult social care workforce strategy – interim statement. London: Department of Health.

Department of Health (2008c) *Good practice in support planning and brokerage: Putting people first personalisation toolkit.* London: Department of Health.

Department of Health (2008d) *Making personal budgets work for older people.* London: Department of Health.

Department of Health (2008e) *Moving forward: Using the learning from the individual budgets pilot. Response to the Ibsen evaluation report from the Department of Health.* London: Department of Health.

Department of Health (2008f) *Refocusing the care programme approach. Policy and positive practice guidance.* London: Department of Health.

Department of Health (2008g) *Safeguarding adults: A consultation on the review of the no secrets guidance.* London: Department of Health.

Department of Health (2009a) *Building a safe, confident future: The final report of the social work task force.* London: Department of Health.

Department of Health (2009b) *New horizons. A shared vision for mental health.* London: Department of Health.

Department of Health (2009c) *Personal health budgets: First steps.* London: Department of Health.

Department of Health (2010a) *Prioritising need in the context of putting people first: A whole system approach to eligibility for social care – guidance on eligibility criteria for adult social care.* London: Department of Health.

Department of Health (2010b) *Fairer contributions guidance: Calculating an individual's contribution to their personal budget.* London: Department of Health.

Department of Health (2010c) *Putting people first: Personal budgets for older people – Making it happen.* London: Department of Health.

Department of Health (2010d) *Putting people first: Support planning and brokerage with older people and people with mental health difficulties.* London: Department of Health.

Department of Health (2010e) *A vision for adult social care: Capable communities and active communities and active citizens.* London: Department of Health.

Department for Work and Pensions (DWP) (2005) *Opportunity age – Meeting the challenges of ageing in the 21st Century.* London: DWP.

Duffy, S (2003) *Keys to citizenship: A guide to getting good support for people with learning disabilities.* Birkenhead: Paradigm.

Duffy, S (2004) In control. *Journal of Integrated Care,* 12 (6): 7–13.

Duffy, S (2006) *Keys to citizenship: A guide to getting good support for people with learning disabilities* (2nd edn). Birkenhead: Paradigm.

Duffy, S (2009) *Self directed support: Social workers contribution paper. Series paper.* London: In Control.

Duffy, S (2010) *New script for care managers: A discussion paper from the Centre of Welfare Reform on behalf of Paradigm and Blackburn with Darwen.* Sheffield: Centre of Welfare Reform.

Duffy, S and Gillespie, J (2009) *Personalisation and safeguarding.* London: In Control.

Dunning, J (2010) *Councils to deny social care support to all but the most needy.* **www.community care.co.uk.**

Edsall, C (1971) *The anti-poor law movement 1834–44.* Manchester: Manchester University Press.

Englander, D (1998) *Poverty and the poor law reform in 19th century Britain 1834–1914: From Chadwick to Booth.* Essex: Longman.

Finnegan, R H (1992) *Oral traditions and the verbal arts: A guide to research practices.* London: Routledge.

Flynn, M (2006) *Developing the role of personal assistants. Researched and compiled for a Skills for Care pilot project examining new and emerging roles in social care.* University of Sheffield, 28 March, LSE.

French, S and Swain, J (2006) Telling stories for a politics of hope. *Disability and Society* 21 (5) 383–97.

Gardner, A (1999) *Making direct payments a reality for people with learning difficulties.* Whalley: North West Training and Development Team.

Glasby, J and Littlechild, R (2009) *Direct payments and personal budgets. Putting personalisation into practice.* Bristol: Policy Press.

Glasby, J, Glendinning, C and Littlechild, R (2006) The future of direct payments, in Leece, J and Bornat, J (eds) *Developments in direct payments.* Bristol: Policy Press.

GSCC (2002) *Code of Practice for social care workers.* London: General Social Care Council.

GSCC (2008) *Social work at its best: A statement of social work roles and tasks for the 21st century.* London: General Social Care Council.

Glendinning, C, Challis, D, Fernandez, J-L, Jacobs, S, Jones, K, Knapp, M, Manthorpe, J, Moran, N, Netten, A, Stevens, M and Wilberforce, M (2008) *Evaluation of the individual budgets pilot programme. Final report.* University of York: Social Policy Research Unit.

Glendinning, C, Arksey, H, Jones, K, Moran, N, Netten, A and Rabiee, P (2009) *The individual budgets pilot projects: Impact and outcomes for carers.* University of York: Social Policy Research Unit; University of Kent: Personal Social Services Research Unit.

Goodley, D (2001) Learning difficulties, the social model of disability and impairment: Challenging epistemologies. *Disability and Society,* 16: 207–31.

Goodley, D, Lawthorn, R, Clough,P and Moore, M (2004) *Researching life stories: Theory and analyses in a biographical age.* London: Routledge Falmer.

Grant, G, Goward, P, Richardson, M,and Ramcharan, R (2005) *Learning disability: A lifestyle approach to valuing people.* Buckingham: Open University Press.

Hasler, F (2006) Holding the dream: direct payments and independent living, in Leece, J and Bornat, J (eds) *Developments in direct payments.* Bristol: Policy Press.

Hatton, C, Waters, J, Duffy, S, Senker, J, Crosby, N, Poll, C, Tyson, A, O'Brien, J and Towell, D (2008) *A report on In control's second phase: Evaluation and learning 2005-2007.* London: In Control.

Henwood, M and Hudson, B (2007) *Here to stay? Self directed support: Aspiration and implementation (a review for the Department of Health).* Heathencote: Melanie Henwood Associates.

Henwood, M and Hudson, B (2008) *Lost to the system? The impact of fair access to care.* London: CSCI.

Henwood, M and Hudson, B (2009) *Keeping it personal: Supporting people with multiple and complex needs. A report to the Commission for Social Care Inspection.* London: CSCI.

Heslop, P and Williams, V (2010a) *Personalisation in mental health: Creating a vision. Views of personalisation from people who use mental health services.* London: Mind.

Heslop, P and Williams, V (2010b) *Personalisation in mental health: Breaking down the barriers. A guide for care co-ordinators.* London: Mind.

Higham, P (2006) *Social work. Introducing professional practice.* London: Sage.

HM Government (2007) *Putting people first: A shared vision and commitment to the transformation of adult social care.* London: Home Office.

HM Government (2010) *The coalition: Our programme for government.* London: HM Government.

HM Treasury and Department for Education and Skills (DfES) (2007) *Aiming high for disabled children: Better support for families.* London: HM Treasury.

Hudson, B (1988) Doomed from the start? *Health Services Journal,* 23 June, 708–9.

In Control (2007) *Making a support plan.* London: In Control.

Independent Living Fund (ILF) (2010) **www.ilf.org.uk**

Jay, D (1937) *The socialist case.* London: Faber and Faber.

Jones, K, Caiels, J, Forder, J, Windle, K, Welch, E, Dolan, P, Glendinning, C and King, D (2010a) *Early experiences of implementing personal health budgets.* PSSRU discussion paper 2726/2. York: SPRU; Kent: PSSRU; London: LSE; London: DH.

Jones, C, Ferguson, I, Lavalette, M and Penketh, L (2010b) *Social work and social justice: A manifesto for a new engaged practice.* **http://socialworkfuture.org.index.php/swan-organisation/manifesto** Accessed 27 October 2010.

Jones, S (2009) *Critical learning for social work students.* Exeter: Learning Matters.

Jordan, B (1974) *Poor parents: Social policy and the 'cycle of deprivation'.* London: Routledge and Kegan Paul.

Kestenbaum, A (1993) *Making community care a reality: The independent living fund, 1988–1993.* London: RADAR.

Leadbeater, C (2004*) Personalisation through participation: A new script for public services.* London: Demos.

Leadbeater, C, Bartlett, J and Gallagher, N (2008) *Making it personal.* London: Demos.

Leece, J and Bornat, B (2006) *Developments in direct payments.* Bristol: Policy Press.

Leece, J and Leece, D (2010) Personalisation: Perceptions of the role of social work in a world of brokers and budgets. *British Journal of Social Work,* Advance Access (published 27 July).

Lewis, J (1995) *The voluntary sector, the state and social work in Britain.* Aldershot: Edward Elgar.

Lombard, D (2010) Personalisation and the social care knowledge gap. *Community Care,* 19 May.

Macintyre, D and Washington, S (2009) *Cash for care abuse warning discussion.* BBC Radio 5 Live, 18 October.

Manthorpe, J, Stevens, M, Rapaport, J, Harns, J, Jacobs, S, Challis, D, Netten, A, Knapp, M, Wilberforce, M and Glendinning, C (2009) Safeguarding and system change: Early perceptions of the implications for adult protection services of the English individual budget pilots. A qualitative study. *British Journal of Social Work,* 39: 1465–80.

Manchester Evening News (2007) *NHS pays for season ticket.* 17 December.

Marks, D (1999) Dimensions of oppression: Theorising the embodied subject. *Disability and Society,* 14: 611–26.

Marsh, P and Fisher, M (1992) *Good intentions: Developing partnership in social services.* York: Joseph Rowntree Foundation.

Marshall, J D (1985) *The old poor law 1795–1834* (2nd edn). London: Macmillan.

Marshall, T (1963) *Sociology at the crossroads.* London: Heinemann.

Marshall, T, and Bottomore, T (1987) *Citizenship and social class.* London: Pluto Press.

McDonald, A (2006) *Understanding community care – a guide for social workers* (2nd edn). Basingstoke: Palgrave Macmillan.

MMU (2009) *Embedding personalisation.* Conference presentation. Manchester Metropolitan University, April 2009.

Morris, J (1993a) Key task 1. Criteria motives. *Community Care*, 14 January: 17.

Morris, J (1993b) Achievable goals. *Community Care*, 18 February: 22–3.

Morris, J (2004) Independent living and community care. A disempowering framework. *Disability and Society*, 19 (5): 427–42.

Mullender, A and Ward, D (1991) *Self directed groupwork – Users take actions for empowerment.* London: Whiting and Birch.

National Institute for Mental Health in England (2006) *Direct payments for people with mental health problems: A guide to action.* Care Services Improvement Partnership (CSIP). London: DH.

National Mental Health Development Unit (NMHDU) (2010) *Paths to personalisation.* London: DH; London: NMHDU.

NCIL (1999) *Government White Paper: Modernising social services – Response by the British Council of Disabled People's National Centre for Independent Living.* London: NCIL.

Newbigging, K with Lowe, J (2005) *Direct payments and mental health: New directions.* Joseph Rowntree Foundation: Pavilion Publishing.

Oliver, M (1990) *The politics of disablement.* Basingstoke: Macmillan.

Oliver, M (2000) Why do insiders matter?, in Moore, M (ed.) *Insider perspectives on inclusion.* Sheffield: Phillip Armstrong Publications.

Oliver, M and Sapey, B (1999) *Social work with disabled people* (2nd edn). Basingstoke: Macmillan.

O'Sullivan, T (1999) *Decision making in social work.* Basingstoke: Macmillan.

Oxford English Dictionary (2005) *Compact Oxford English Dictionary of Current English* (3rd edn). Oxford: Oxford University Press.

Parker, J (2010) *Effective practice learning in social work* (2nd edn). Exeter: Learning Matters.

Payne, M (1995) *Social work and community care.* Basingstoke: Macmillan.

Poll, C, Duffy, S, Hatton, C, Sanderson, H and Routledge, M (2006) *A report on In Control's first phase 2003–2005.* London: In Control Publications.

Powell, M and Hewitt, M (2002) *Welfare state and welfare change.* Buckingham: Open University Press.

Prabhakar, M, Thom, G, Hurstfield. J and Parashar, U (2008) *Individual budgets for families with disabled children. Scoping Study. Research report no. DCSF-RRO57.* SQW Consulting.

Prabhakar, M, Thom, G and Johnson, R (2010) *Individual budgets for families with disabled children – Interim report 2010. Research report DFE – RRO24.* SQW Consulting.

Priestley, M (2004) Tragedy strikes again! Why community care still poses a problem for integrated living, in Swain, J, French, S, Barnes, C and Thomas, C (eds) *Disabling barriers – Enabling environments.* London: Sage.

Prime Minister's Strategy Unit (2005) *Improving the life chances of disabled people.* London: Cabinet Office.

Pugh, R, Scharf, T, Williams, C and Roberts, D (2007) Research Briefing 22. *Obstacles to using and providing rural social care.* London: Social Care Institute for Excellence.

Putting People First (2009) *Transforming adult social care: Putting people first toolkit.* London Borough of Newham: Putting People First. **www.puttingpeoplefirst.org.uk**

Rabiee, P, Moran, N and Glendinning, C (2009) Individual budgets: Lessons from early users' experiences. *British Journal of Social Work*, 39: 918–35.

Renshaw, C (2008) Do self assessment and self directed support undermine traditional social work with disabled people? *Disability and Society*, 23 (3): 283–86.

Ridley, J and Jones, L (2003) Direct what? The untapped potential of direct payments to mental health service users. *Disability and Society*, 18 (5): 643–58.

RIPRA (2008) *Support brokerage, key issues 02.* Totnes: Research in Practice for Adults.

Sandel, M (2010) *Justice: What's the right thing to do?* London: Penguin Group.

Sanderson, H (2000) *Person centred planning: Key features and approaches.* York: Joseph Rowntree Foundation.

Schön, D (1986) *Educating the reflective practitioner.* Oxford: Jossey-Bass.

Scourfield, P (2010) Going for brokerage: A task of independent support or social work? *British Journal of Social Work*, 40 (3): 868–77.

Shardlow, S and Nelson, P (eds) (2005) *Introducing social work.* Lyme Regis: Russell House.

Smale, G, Tuson, G, Biehal, N. and Marsh, P (1993) *Empowerment, assessment, care management and the skilled worker.* London: NISW/HMSO.

Spandler, H (2004) Friend or foe? Towards a critical assessment of direct payments. *Critical Social Policy*, 24 (2): 187–209.

Smith, B and Sparkes, A (2005) Men, sport, spinal cord injury and narratives of hope. *Social Science and Medicine*, 61: 1095–105.

Smith, B and Sparkes, A (2008) Narrative and its potential contribution to disability studies. *Disability and Society*, 23 (1): 17–28.

Social Care Institute for Excellence (2009) *At a glance 18: Personalisation briefing. Implications for community mental health services.* London: SCIE.

Social Exclusion Unit (2004) *Mental health and social exclusion: Social Exclusion Unit Report.* London: Office of the Deputy Prime Minister.

Stuart, O (2006) *SCIE Race equality discussion paper 01: Will community based support services make direct payments a viable option for black and minority ethnic service users and carers?* London: Social Care Institute for Excellence.

Swain, J, Finklestein, V, French, S and Oliver, M (eds) (1993) *Disabling barriers – Enabling environments.* London: Sage Publications in association with the Open University.

Thomas, C (1999) Narrative identity and the disabled self, in Corker, M and French, S (eds) *Disability and discourse.* Milton Keynes: Open University Press.

Thompson, N (2005) *Understanding social work: Preparing for practice* (2nd edn). Basingstoke: Palgrave Macmillan.

Thompson, N (2006) *Anti-discriminatory practice.* Basingstoke: Palgrave Macmillan.

Thompson, N (2009) *Understanding social work: Preparing for practice* (3rd edn). Basingstoke: Palgrave Macmillan.

Todd, L (2006) Enabling practice for professionals: The need for post-structuralist theory, in Goodley, D and Lawthorn, R (eds) *Disability and psychology*. Basingstoke: Palgrave Macmillan.

Topss England (2002) *National occupational standards for social work.* **www.topssengland.net**

Tyson, A (2009) *Self-directed support: Social workers contribution.* London: In Control.

Tyson, A, Brewis, R, Crosby, N, Hatton, C, Stansfield, J, Tomlinson, C, Waters, J and Wood, A (2010) *A report on In Control's third phase: Evaluation and learning 2008–2009.* London: In Control.

UPIAS (1976) *Fundamental principles of disability.* London: UPIAS.

Unison (2010) *Who cares: Who pays? Report on personalisation.* London: Unison.

Unison Eastern (2009) *Social workers – personalised budget.* **www.unisoneastern.org.uk**

Walton, P (1999) Social work and mental health: refocusing the training agenda for ASWs. *Social Work Education*, 18 (4): 375–88.

Wilson, R and Gilbert, K (2006) An experience of direct payments development fund, in Leece, J and Bornat, J (eds) *Developments in direct payments.* Bristol: Policy Press.

Wolfensberger, W (1972) *The principle of normalization in human services.* Toronto: National Institute on Mental Retardation.

Wolfensberger, W (1983) Social role valorization: A proposed new term for the principle of normalization. *Mental Retardation*, 21 (6): 234–39.

Zarb, G and Nadesh, P (1994) *Cashing in on independence: Comparing the costs and benefits of cash and services.* London: British Council of Disabled People (BCODP).

Website

www.supportplanning.org.uk, 2006 Thinking about support planning. London: Support planning.

Index

Added to the page reference 'g' denotes the glossary.

Transforming Social Work Practice – titles in the series

Applied Psychology for Social Work (second edition)	ISBN 978 1 84445 356 6
Assessment in Social Work Practice	ISBN 978 1 84445 293 4
Collaborative Social Work Practice	ISBN 978 1 84445 014 5
Communication and Interpersonal Skills in Social Work (third edition)	ISBN 978 1 84445 610 9
Courtroom Skills for Social Workers	ISBN 978 1 84445 123 4
Critical Learning for Social Work Students	ISBN 978 1 84445 201 9
Effective Practice Learning in Social Work (second edition)	ISBN 978 1 84445 253 8
Effective Writing Skills for Social Work Students	ISBN 978 0 85725 417 7
Equality and Diversity in Social Work Practice	ISBN 978 1 84445 593 5
Groupwork Practice in Social Work (second edition)	ISBN 978 1 85725 502 0
Interprofessional Social Work: Effective Collaborative Approaches (second edition)	ISBN 978 1 84445 379 5
Introducing International Social Work	ISBN 978 1 84445 132 6
Loss and Social Work	ISBN 978 1 84445 088 6
Management and Organisations in Social Work (second edition)	ISBN 978 1 84445 216 3
Need, Risk and Protection in Social Work Practice	ISBN 978 1 84445 252 1
New Directions in Social Work Practice	ISBN 978 1 84445 079 4
Personalisation in Social Work	ISBN 978 1 84445 732 8
Practical Computer Skills for Social Work	ISBN 978 1 84445 031 2
Proactive Child Protection and Social Work	ISBN 978 1 84445 131 9
Reflective Practice in Social Work (second edition)	ISBN 978 1 84445 364 1
Research Skills for Social Work	ISBN 978 1 84445 179 1
Safeguarding Adults in Social Work (second edition)	ISBN 978 0 85725 401 6
Sensory Awareness and Social Work	ISBN 978 1 84445 293 4
Service User and Carer Participation in Social Work	ISBN 978 1 84445 074 9
Sexuality and Social Work	ISBN 978 1 84445 085 5
Social Policy and Social Work	ISBN 978 1 84445 301 6
Social Work and Human Development (third edition)	ISBN 978 1 84445 380 1
Social Work and Mental Health (fourth edition)	ISBN 978 0 85725 493 1

Social Work and Mental Health in Scotland	ISBN 978 1 84445 130 2
Social Work and Spirituality	ISBN 978 1 84445 194 4
Social Work in Education and Children's Services	ISBN 978 1 84445 045 9
Social Work Intervention	ISBN 978 1 84445 199 9
Social Work Practice: Assessment, Planning, Intervention and Review (third edition)	ISBN 978 1 84445 831 8
Social Work Skills with Adults	ISBN 978 1 84445 218 7
Social Work Skills with Children, Young People and their Families	ISBN 978 1 84445 346 7
Social Work with Children and Families (second edition)	ISBN 978 1 84445 144 9
Social Work with Children, Young People and their Families in Scotland (second edition)	ISBN 978 1 84445 156 2
Social Work with Drug and Substance Misusers (second edition)	ISBN 978 1 84445 262 0
Social Work with Looked After Children	ISBN 978 1 84445 103 6
Social Work with Older People (second edition)	ISBN 978 1 84445 155 5
Social Work with People with Learning Difficulties (second edition)	ISBN 978 1 84445 042 8
Sociology and Social Work	ISBN 978 1 84445 087 9
Studying for your Social Work Degree (second edition)	ISBN 978 0 85725 381 1
Thriving and Surviving in Social Work	ISBN 978 1 84445 080 0
Understanding and Using Theory in Social Work (second edition)	ISBN 978 0 85725 497 9
Using the Law in Social Work (fifth edition)	ISBN 978 0 85725 405 4
Values and Ethics in Social Work (second edition)	ISBN 978 1 84445 370 2
What is Social Work? Context and Perspectives (third edition)	ISBN 978 1 84445 248 4
Working with Aggression and Resistance in Social Work	ISBN 978 0 85725 4 290
Youth Justice and Social Work (second edition)	ISBN 978 0 85725 319 4

To order, please contact our distributor: BEBC Distribution, Albion Close, Parkstone, Poole, BH12 3LL. Telephone: 0845 230 9000, email: **learningmatters@bebc.co.uk**. You can also find more information on each of these titles and our other learning resources at www.learningmatters.co.uk